CUSTOM WOODEN MUSIC BOXES

FOR THE SCROLL SAW

BY RICK AND KAREN LONGABAUGH

Fox
Chapel Publishing

1970 Broad Street • East Petersburg, PA 17520
www.FoxChapelPublishing.com

Bibliographical note
Custom Wooden Music Boxes for the Scroll Saw is a revised and expanded republication of *Holiday Scrollsaw Music Boxes*, originally published in 1999, and *Victorian Scrollsaw Music Boxes*, originally published in 2000. This edition of the work includes expanded instructions with full-color photos for getting started, along with full-color photos of a selection of the finished projects.

ISBN-13: 978–1–56523–301–0
ISBN-10: 1–56523–301–8

Publisher's Cataloging-in-Publication Data

Longabaugh, Rick.

　　Custom wooden music boxes for the scroll saw / by Rick and Karen
　　Longabaugh. -- East Petersburg, PA : Fox Chapel Publishing,
　　c2006.

　　　　p. ; cm.

　　　　ISBN-13: 978-1-56523-301-0
　　　　ISBN-10: 1-56523-301-8
　　　　Rev. and expanded ed. of: Holiday scrollsaw music boxes,
　　originally published in 1999, and: Victorian scrollsaw music boxes,
　　originally published in 2000.

　　　　1. Music box--Construction. 2. Wood-carving--Technique.
　　3. Wood-carving--Patterns. 4. Jig saws. I. Longabaugh, Karen.
　　II. Title. III. Holiday scrollsaw music boxes. IV. Victorian scrollsaw
　　music boxes.
　　TT199.7 .L66 2006
　　736/.4--dc22　　　　　　　　　　　　　　　　　　0604

Printed in China
10 9 8 7 6 5 4 3 2 1

To learn more about the other great books from Fox Chapel Publishing,
or to find a retailer near you, call toll-free 1-800-457-9112 or visit us at
www.FoxChapelPublishing.com.

Note to Authors: We are always looking for talented authors to write new books in our area of woodworking, design, and related crafts. Please send a brief letter describing your idea to Peg Couch, Acquisition Editor, 1970 Broad Street, East Petersburg, PA 17520.

Alan Giagnocavo
Publisher

Peg Couch
Acquisition Editor

Gretchen Bacon
Editor

Troy Thorne
Cover Design & Layout

TABLE OF CONTENTS

Rick and Karen Longabaugh started The Berry
Basket and Great American Scrollsaw Patterns—
their online and mail order company, specializing
in unique and useful scroll saw patterns and accessories—
in the fall of 1990. What began as one set of collapsible
basket patterns became a complete line of full-size
woodworking patterns and hard-to-find accessories.

Rick has been featured on the popular PBS show *The
American Woodshop* with Scott Phillips and also on the
cover of *Popular Woodworking* magazine. Many of their
unique projects have been published in a number of
woodworking publications, including *Wood* magazine,
Creative Woodworks & Crafts, *Popular Woodworking*, *The
Art of the Scroll Saw*, *Scroll Saw Workshop*, and Patrick
Spielman's *Home Workshop News*.

To find materials and supplies for scroll sawing, contact
The Berry Basket, PO Box 925, Centralia, WA 98531,
1–800–206–9009, **www.berrybasket.com**.

INTRODUCTION

For over 200 years, music boxes have fascinated and enchanted millions of people the world over. Antoine Favre, a watchmaker from Geneva, Switzerland, invented the first mechanical musical movement in 1796. The industry stayed centered in Geneva until 1811 when it moved to the village of Sainte-Croix, Switzerland, where the tradition lives on to this day. The most famous and world-renowned manufacturer from this area is Reuge Music, which produces the beautifully toned Romance Musical Movements.

In 1996, The Berry Basket started a music box tradition of its own. Designing the first of hundreds of scroll saw music box patterns to come, renowned scroll saw artist Rick Longabaugh created a beautifully animated Christmas nativity. From the overwhelming response this first pattern received came new patterns for angels, horses, Santas, snowmen, and more. We gathered the patterns together in this unique pattern book, which will show you how easy it is to create beautiful animated keepsakes that will be treasured for generations to come. With instructions and full-size patterns, you'll be creating enchanting scrolled music boxes with professional results in no time at all.

The following scroll saw tips and techniques are intended to get you started and on your way to scroll saw success. You will find these techniques helpful in completing the projects in this book as well as other scroll saw projects.

SAFETY TIPS

Always keep safety in mind as you are working. Here are some general safety guidelines to take into consideration before you begin.

- Use glasses, goggles, or similar equipment to protect your eyes.

- Remove any loose clothing or jewelry before you operate your saw.

- It is always a good idea to work in a well-ventilated area. Consider using a mask, an air cleaner, a dust collector, or any combination of these to protect your lungs from fine dust.

- Be sure that your work area is well lighted.

- Keep your hands a safe distance away from the blade.

- Don't work when you are tired or unfocused.

COPYING THE PATTERN

The patterns contained in this book are intended to be your master patterns. We recommend making photocopies of the project pieces and then using a repositionable spray adhesive to adhere them to your workpiece. This method of transfer is easier, less time-consuming, and far more accurate than tracing. Using a photocopier will also allow you to enlarge or reduce the pattern to fit the size of wood you choose to use. Please note that some photocopy machines may cause a slight distortion in size, so it is important to use the same photocopier for all of the pieces of your project and to photocopy your patterns in the same direction. Distortion is more likely to occur on very large patterns.

Figure 1. Be sure to sand the workpiece before applying the pattern. You may also want to sand the wood lightly once you have cut the design and removed the pattern to eliminate any "fuzz" and to get rid of any glue residue.

PREPARING THE SURFACE

For most projects, it is best to sand the workpiece prior to applying the paper pattern and cutting the design (see **Figure 1**). Once you've cut the design and removed the paper pattern, it may be necessary to lightly sand off any glue residue remaining, along with any "fuzz" on the bottom side.

TRANSFERRING THE PATTERN

Using a repositionable spray adhesive is the easiest and quickest way to transfer a pattern to your workpiece after photocopying it. (These adhesives can be found at most arts and crafts, photography, and department stores. Pay special attention to purchase one that states "temporary bond" or "repositionable.")

Start by setting up in a well-ventilated area. Lightly spray the back side of the paper pattern, not the wood (see **Figure 2**). Allow it to dry only until tacky—approximately 20 to 30 seconds. Then, apply it to the workpiece, smoothing out any wrinkles if necessary.

One of the most common problems with using repositionable spray adhesive for the first time is applying the right amount onto the back of the pattern. Spraying too little may result in the pattern's lifting off the project while you are cutting. If this occurs, clear Scotch tape or 2" clear packaging tape can be used to secure the pattern back into position. Spraying too much will make it difficult to remove the pattern. If this occurs, simply use a handheld hair dryer to heat the glue, which will loosen the pattern and allow it to be easily removed.

SELECTING THE MATERIALS

Selecting the type of material that you will use is very important for the final outcome of your project. Although plywood could be used for many of the music box projects contained in this book, we highly recommend choosing any of the beautiful hardwoods available (see **Figure 3**). The elegant nature of these heirloom-quality projects is far more impressive with the creative use of contrasting hardwoods. Mixing dark woods, such as walnut and mahogany, with light woods, such as maple and birch, will produce the most striking effect.

If you are relatively new to scrolling, we recommend using a high-quality Baltic birch plywood for cutting pieces, such as overlays, figures, tops, bottoms, and turntables. Baltic birch plywood is easier to use than hardwoods and can be stained for color contrast.

Figure 2. Use "repositionable" spray adhesive to adhere your patterns to the wood. A simple glue box, made from a common cardboard box, helps to confine the adhesive.

Figure 3. Hardwoods offer a variety of colors and grain patterns that can enhance your projects. Shown here from left to right are catalpa, red oak, cherry, birch, black walnut, white oak, mahogany, and American aromatic cedar.

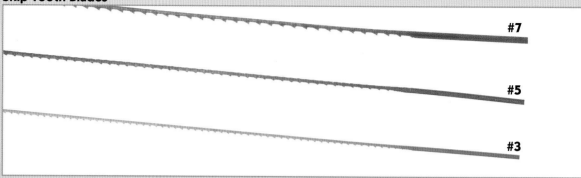

#7

#5

#3

Figure 4. Skip tooth blades can be good blades for a beginning scroller. Pictured here from bottom to top are skip tooth blades #3, #5, and #7.

SELECTING THE BLADE

There are many opinions regarding which blade to use, depending on which type and thickness of material you choose and on how intricate the design in the project is. The more time you put into scrolling, the more your choice of which blade to use will become personal preference.

For the beginning scroller, we recommend skip tooth blades, but be sure to experiment and find the blade that suits you best (see **Figure 4**). We also offer the following blade size guidelines to get you started:

Material Thickness	Blade Size Recommended
1/16" to 1/4"	#2/0, #2, or #3
1/4" to 1/2"	#5 or #7
1/2" to 3/4" or thicker	#7 or #9

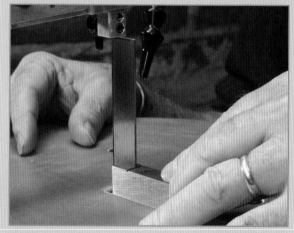

Figure 5. One way to check if your table is square to your blade is to use a small square. Place the square next to the blade and adjust the table as necessary until the blade and the square are parallel.

SQUARING THE BLADE

Before you begin cutting, it's a good idea to check that your table is square to the blade. Lift the saw arm up to its highest point and place a 2" triangle or a small square beside the blade (see **Figure 5**). If the blade and the square aren't parallel to each other, adjust your table until both the blade and the square line up.

If you don't have a square or triangle, try this method using a piece of scrap wood. First, make a small cut in a piece of scrap wood (see **Figure 6**). Then, turn the scrap wood until the cut is facing the back of the blade. Slide the wood across the table so that the blade fits into the cut. If the blade inserts easily into the cut, it is square. If the blade does not insert easily into the cut, adjust the table until the blade is square.

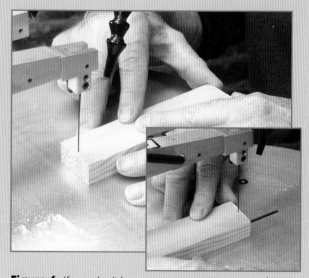

Figure 6. If you don't have a square, you can use a piece of scrap wood to square the table to the blade. First, make a small cut in the piece of scrap wood. Then, slide the cut toward the blade from the back. If the blade fits into the cut easily, the table is square to the blade.

Figure 7. Drill any blade entry holes after adhering the pattern to the wood. Locate the blade entry holes close to corners so that it will take less time for the blade to reach the pattern line.

CREATING AN AUXILIARY TABLE

Most scroll saws on the market today have an opening in the table and around the blade that is much larger than is necessary. This design often causes small and delicate fretwork to break off on the downward stroke of the blade. An easy solution is to add a wooden auxiliary table to the top of the metal table on your saw.

To make an auxiliary table, choose a piece of ¼" to ⅜" plywood that is similar to the size of your current saw's table. If you wish, you can cut this plywood to the same shape as the metal table on your saw, or to any shape or size you prefer. We do recommend, however, that you make the table larger than what you think you will need for the size of the projects you will make in the future.

Next, set the auxiliary table on top of the metal table. From the underside of the metal table, use a pencil to mark the location where the blade will feed through. Then, turn the auxiliary table over and drill a ¹⁄₁₆"- to ⅛"-diameter hole, or a hole slightly larger than the blade you will be using.

Finally, apply a few strips of double-sided carpet tape to the metal table on each side of the blade. Firmly press the auxiliary table onto the double-sided carpet tape, making sure that the blade is centered in the hole.

DRILLING BLADE ENTRY HOLES

If your project requires blade entry holes, be sure to drill all of them once you have adhered the paper pattern to the workpiece with repositionable spray adhesive. When drilling blade entry holes, it is best to drill close to a corner, rather than in the middle of the waste areas, because it will take less time for the blade to reach the pattern line (see **Figure 7**). Sand the back of the piece to remove any burrs before you begin cutting.

VEINING

Veining is a simple technique that will bring a lifelike appearance to your project. The veins of a leaf or the folds of clothing will look more realistic when this technique is applied.

To vein, simply choose a thin blade (usually smaller than #7) and saw all solid black lines, as indicated on the pattern. You will be able to vein some areas of the pattern by sawing inward from the outside edge (see **Figure 8**); in other areas, you will need to drill a tiny blade entry hole for the blade.

If you wish to make a project easier, simply omit the veining.

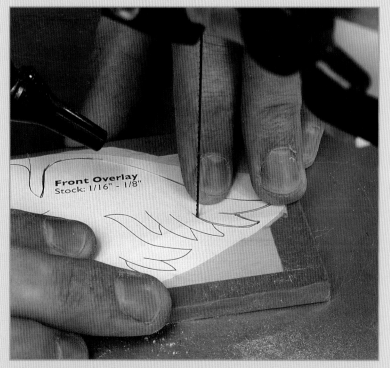

Figure 8. Veining can give your projects a lifelike appearance. Many times veining areas will be as simple as cutting inward from the outside edge.

CUTTING THE FRAME

Cutting the 1½"-thick frame will probably be the most challenging part of these projects. Using the proper size of scroll saw blade will make this step easier. A universal #9 (or larger) blade is highly recommended. This will make cutting quicker and more accurate. Also, depending upon the type of wood you are using for the frame, you may want to consider using a double skip tooth or a precision blade.

Using a band saw with a ¹⁄₁₆" to ⅛" blade for cutting the outside shape is another way to make this part of the process easier. Note that the more teeth per inch on the blade, the smoother the cut will be.

Another alternative for cutting the frame is to cut two ¾"-thick pieces of wood separately, and then secure them together with wood screws or glue. To start, adhere the paper frame pattern to one of the ¾"-thick workpieces. Cut the outer

shape and opening for the music box movement, following the solid lines. Then, countersink in two locations for #6 x 1¼" F.H. wood screws, being careful not to countersink where indicated for attaching the bottom to the frame. Secure this half of the frame to the remaining ¾"-thick workpiece with the #6 screws. Next, trace the shape of the top frame half onto the bottom half workpiece (see **Figure 9**). Remove the screws and separate the two halves. Cut the bottom half on the solid line; then reattach the two halves together with the screws, and sand where they meet until the area is flush (see **Figure 10**).

This method also allows you the opportunity to add a decorative touch to the middle area of the frame. Prior to reattaching the two halves of the frame, use a roundover or a beading bit where the two halves meet.

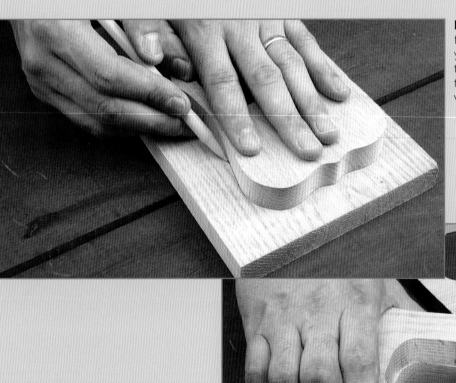

Figure 9. If you don't have 1½" wood for the frame, use two pieces of ¾"-thick wood. Once you have cut the first frame piece, attach it to the second piece of wood with screws. Then, trace the shape of the frame onto the bottom workpiece.

Figure 10. Once both pieces have been cut, line them up, attach them with screws, and sand the area where they meet until it is flush.

CUTTING THE FEET

Several of the patterns contained in this book require two or more feet. Here is a simple procedure that produces decorative wooden feet to elegantly support your music box treasure. Please see the Customizing Your Project section on page 10 for additional foot ideas.

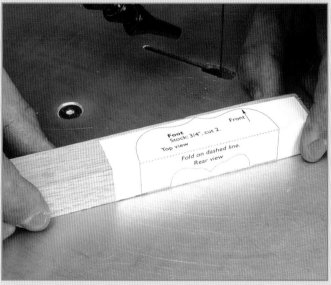

1. Prior to applying the spray adhesive to the back of the feet pattern, fold the pattern where indicated on the dashed lines. Then, spray the pattern with the adhesive and apply it to the workpiece.

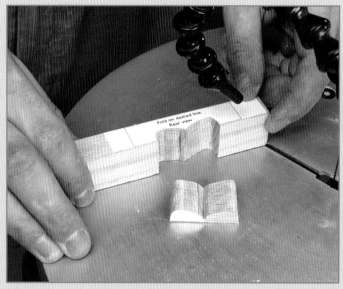

2. Turn the workpiece upright so that the portion of the pattern marked "Rear view" is facing up. Then, cut on the solid line.

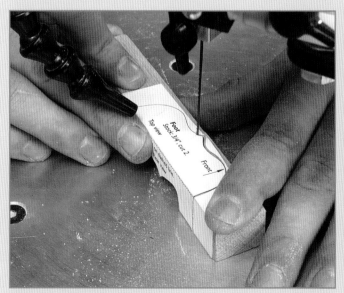

3. Next, turn the workpiece so that the "Top view" is facing up. Cut following the solid line.

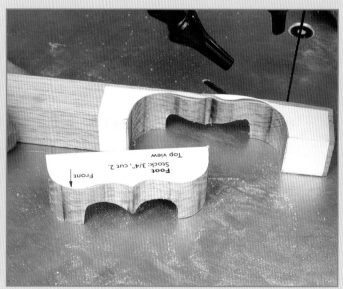

4. Release the piece from the block. Then, remove the paper pattern, sand as needed, and attach the feet where indicated on the project.

STACK CUTTING

Stack cutting is fairly simple to do and can save you a lot of time when you have two or more identical pieces to cut for a project or if you are making more than one of a particular project. If you are fairly new to scroll sawing and stack cutting, we recommend cutting no more than a total thickness of ½" for best results.

On projects with fairly simple shapes, two or three layers could be held together by double-sided tape or by paper sprayed on both sides with repositionable adhesive and sandwiched between the workpieces. You could also put masking tape on each edge of the stack to hold the pattern and the workpieces in place (see **Figure 11**).

On more intricate projects, we suggest using #18 wire nails or brads that are slightly longer than the total thickness of the stack you are cutting. Tack the nails into the waste areas you will cut out, along with a few around the outside of the project. If the nail has gone through the bottom of the workpiece, use a hammer to tap it flush or use coarse sandpaper to sand the points flush with the bottom of the workpiece.

If you are stack cutting hardwoods, do not tack the nail too close to the pattern line or it may cause the wood to split. You could also predrill holes for the nails with a slightly smaller drill bit so the nail will fit snugly and hold the layers together securely.

SAWING THIN WOODS

Thin hardwoods or plywoods can be difficult to work with because they're prone to breaking. The following suggestions should help to eliminate or reduce this problem.

- If you have a variable speed saw, reduce the speed to ½ to ¾ of high speed.
- If you do not have a variable speed saw, it will help to stack cut two or more layers of material to prevent breakage.
- For cutting any thickness of material, it is very beneficial to keep the fingers of at least one hand, if not both, partially touching the table for better control (see **Figure 12**).
- With any material, it is important that your feed rate and blade speed match so that burn marks won't appear on the wood. If you prefer to feed the wood into the blade slowly, set your saw on a slow setting or try using a smaller blade with more teeth per inch to slow down the speed at which the blade is cutting. On the other hand, if you prefer to feed the wood into the blade quickly, choose a fast setting for your saw or try using a blade with fewer teeth per inch.

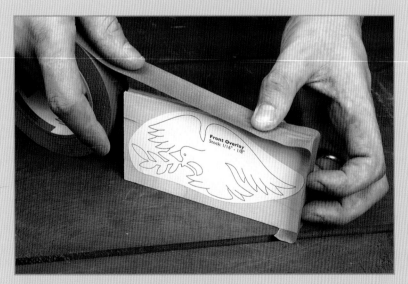

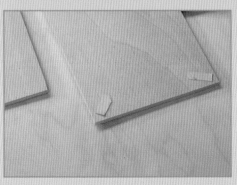

Figure 11. Masking tape or painter's tape (shown) placed around the edges can be used to hold a stack together. Some scrollers also like to cover the surface of the wood with tape before adhering the pattern to help lubricate the blade as it cuts. Placing double-sided tape in the corners of the stack can also be an effective method of holding the stack together.

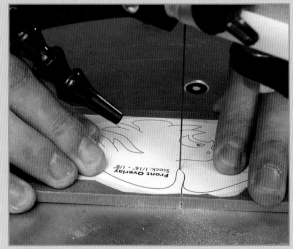

Figure 12. Keeping some of the fingers of both hands in contact with the surface can give you better control.

Figure 13. The music box movement and components you choose will depend on personal taste and on what is available in your area. Pictured here, clockwise from the top, is a music box movement, a turntable, a key, and an extender.

Figure 14. Attach the frame to the base. Due to the style of our music box, we attached the back cover to the front of the frame.

MUSIC BOX MOVEMENT KIT

A music box movement (tune), metal turntable, and key are required to animate the projects in this book (see **Figure 13**). For information on suppliers, please see the Resources section on page 188.

The proper length of shafts are 18mm for the key and 28mm for the metal turntable disc. If a retailer does not offer these lengths, you may need to purchase an extender that will give you the proper length, or close to it. It is better to choose a length slightly larger than needed to be sure that there is enough clearance for winding without scraping the wood surface.

The projects in this book are designed to use traditional-style movements (where a key winds it from the bottom and a metal turntable disc attaches the wooden turntable to the top side). However, other movement styles can be used with a slight modification to the pattern/project to ensure that the movement and turntable are properly aligned. Before cutting the opening in the frame for the music box movement, compare the size and shape of the movement's bottom to the solid line on the paper pattern to see that they match. Also check to be sure that the winding shaft is in the proper location. If the opening indicated on the pattern and the actual movement do not match, trace around the movement to mark the cutout section for that movement. In some cases, the movement's bottom can be sanded to fit the opening. You might also consider using a 2¾"-diameter Forstner bit or a hole saw to bore the hole into the frame for the music box movement rather than cutting it.

Figure 15. Attach the metal turntable to the wood turntable and thread the metal turntable onto the music box shaft.

If you have already cut the frame prior to purchasing a musical movement, you may simply need to flip the frame end-to-end or top-to-bottom. If not, it may be necessary to recut the opening for the movement, or even the frame itself.

ASSEMBLY FOR VERTICAL TURNTABLE PROJECTS

Assemble by first attaching the back cover to the back of the frame. Then, attach this assembly to the base (see **Figure 14**). Next, insert the music box, securing with screws or silicone. Use silicone to attach the metal turntable to the back of the wood turntable. Then, thread the metal turntable onto the music box shaft (see **Figure 15**). Attach the overlays and the arch or supports where indicated, using glue or silicone to secure. Next, attach the front cover to the base. If your type of movement has places for a key and a turntable, thread the key into position. **Note:** If using silicone, be careful not to use too much because it may squeeze out from between the two pieces and get into the movement itself.

ASSEMBLY FOR HORIZONTAL TURNTABLE PROJECTS

First, attach the top to the frame with glue and finishing nails or silicone. Next, attach the music box movement to the topside of the bottom with screws or silicone (depending on the type of movement you choose, you may need to attach the movement differently). Before the silicone sets, position the frame over the bottom to make sure the music box movement is aligned correctly (see **Figure 16**). Then, secure the bottom to the frame. Attach the metal turntable to the bottom of the wood turntable with silicone and attach the figure to the top (see **Figure 17**). Next, attach the turntable and key to the music box (if your movement has room for only a turntable or a key, attach the turntable). Finally, attach the arch, feet, overlays, or figures, securing with glue or silicone (see **Figure 18**). **Note:** If using silicone, be careful not to use too much because it may squeeze out from between the two pieces and get into the movement itself.

FINISHING TECHNIQUES

Finishing can be done before or after assembling. For many pieces, especially those with a fair amount of fretwork, it is easier to apply the finish prior to assembling. If you finish the piece before assembling, you also have more options for using contrasting stains.

If you made your project from hardwood, we recommend dipping it in a dishpan (or a similar container) filled with a penetrating oil, such as Watco or tung. Then, allow the excess oil to drain back into the pan, and follow the manufacturer's instructions.

If you have chosen to use plywood on any parts of your project, try using a matching shade of stain to give an appealing look to the finished project.

As a final finish step once the pieces have dried, use a clear, Varathane-type spray for a protective coating.

CUSTOMIZING YOUR PROJECT

Many of the overlays, figures, turntables, and feet in this book are designed to be interchangeable with each other. Options for the feet can also include using decorative wooden finials, portions of axle pegs, spindles, or smokestacks, as well as brass, metal, or porcelain pull knobs designed for drawers or furniture. Use your imagination and be creative in customizing your own music box masterpiece.

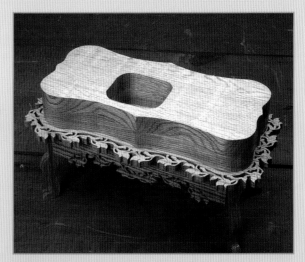

Figure 16. Set the frame in place to be sure that the music box movement is aligned correctly.

Figure 17. Attach the metal turntable to the wood and attach the figure to the top of the wood. Then, screw the turntable into the music box movement. Our movement had room for only a key or a turntable, so we will use the turntable to wind the movement.

Figure 18. Once the turntable is in place, assemble the rest of the music box.

ANGELS

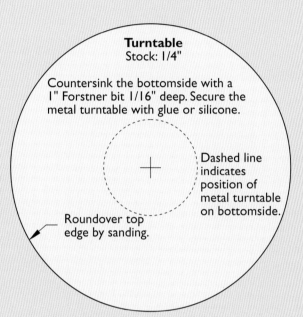

Turntable
Stock: 1/4"

Countersink the bottomside with a 1" Forstner bit 1/16" deep. Secure the metal turntable with glue or silicone.

Dashed line indicates position of metal turntable on bottomside.

Roundover top edge by sanding.

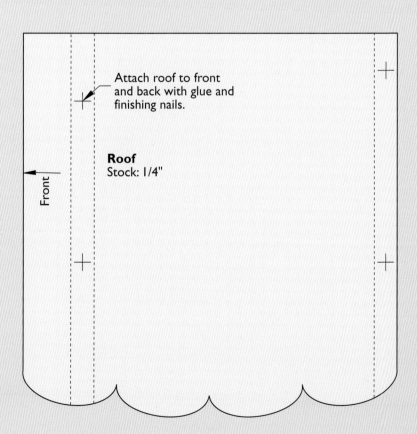

Attach roof to front and back with glue and finishing nails.

Roof
Stock: 1/4"

Front

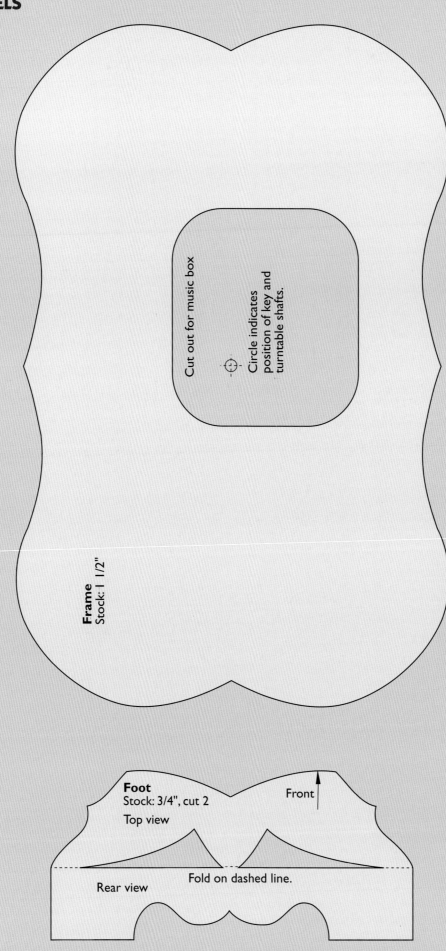

Cut out for music box

Circle indicates
position of key and
turntable shafts.

Frame
Stock: 1 1/2"

Foot
Stock: 3/4", cut 2
Top view

Front

Fold on dashed line.

Rear view

A Joyful Noise

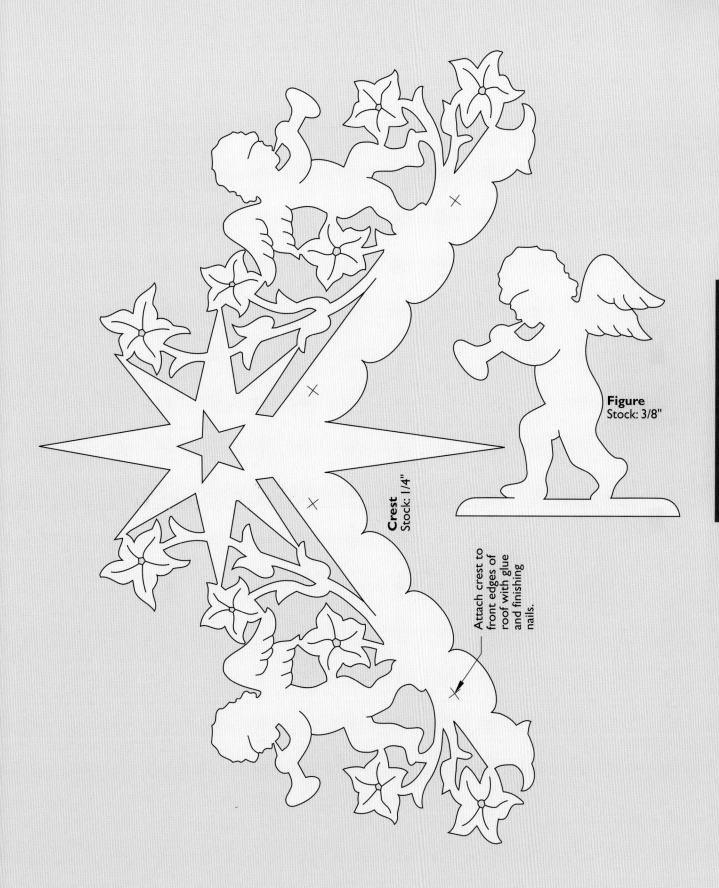

Crest
Stock: 1/4"

Figure
Stock: 3/8"

Attach crest to front edges of roof with glue and finishing nails.

A Joyful Noise

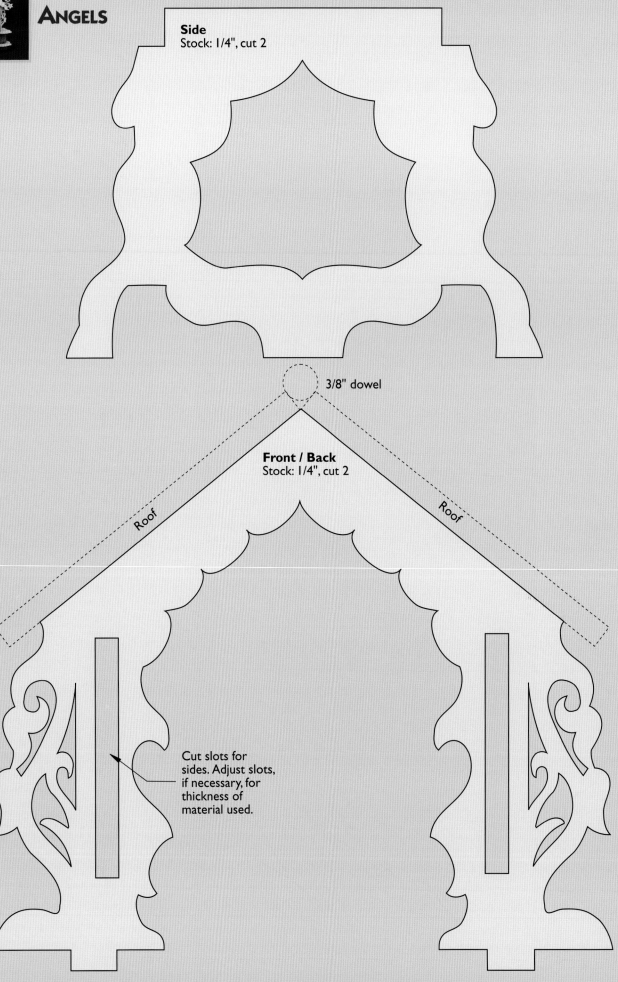

Side
Stock: 1/4", cut 2

3/8" dowel

Roof

Roof

Front / Back
Stock: 1/4", cut 2

Cut slots for
sides. Adjust slots,
if necessary, for
thickness of
material used.

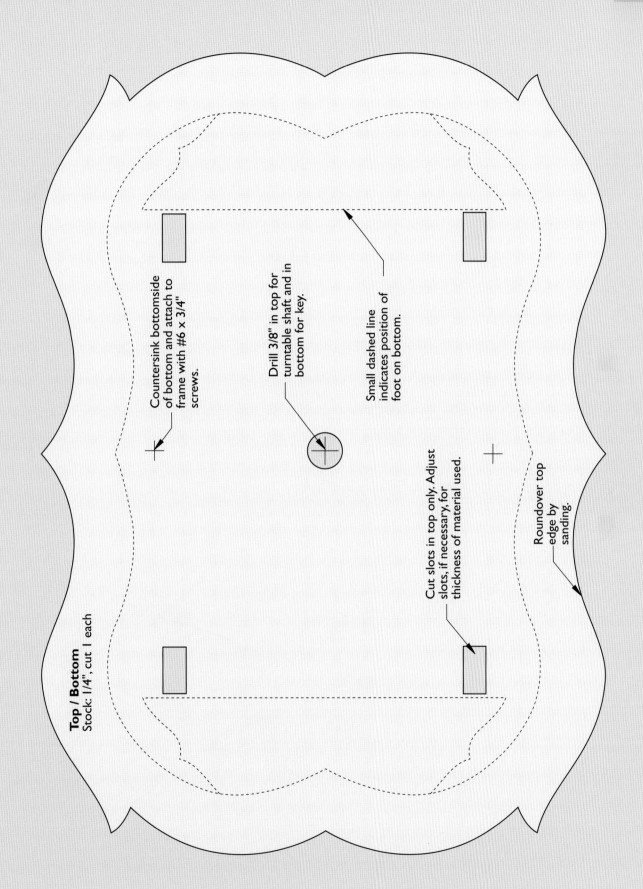

Countersink bottomside of bottom and attach to frame with #6 x 3/4" screws.

Drill 3/8" in top for turntable shaft and in bottom for key.

Small dashed line indicates position of foot on bottom.

Cut slots in top only. Adjust slots, if necessary, for thickness of material used.

Roundover top edge by sanding.

Top / Bottom
Stock: 1/4", cut 1 each

A Joyful Noise

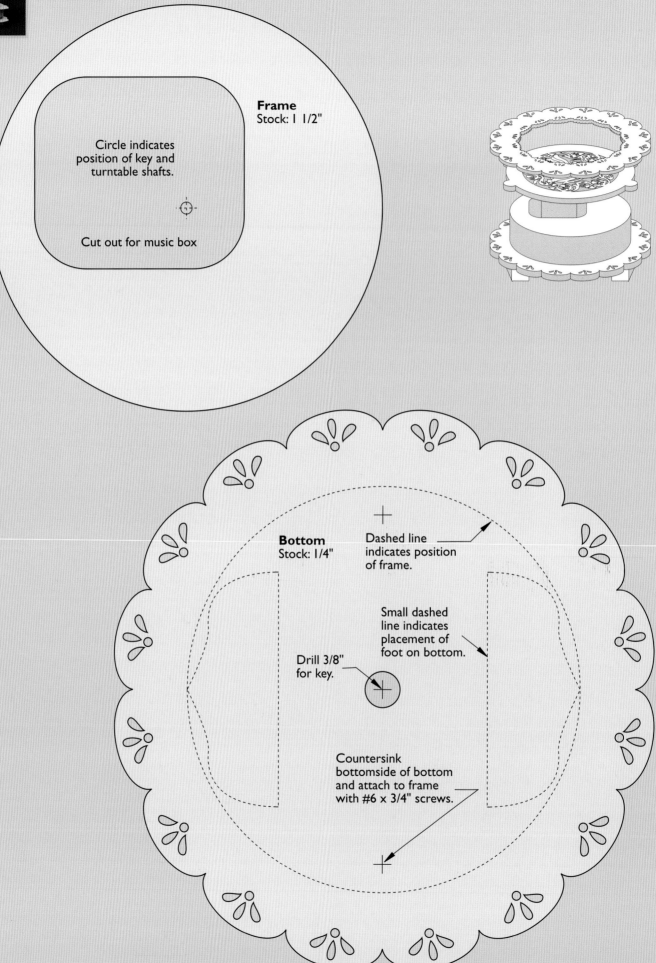

Frame
Stock: 1 1/2"

Circle indicates
position of key and
turntable shafts.

Cut out for music box

Bottom
Stock: 1/4"

Dashed line
indicates position
of frame.

Small dashed
line indicates
placement of
foot on bottom.

Drill 3/8"
for key.

Countersink
bottomside of bottom
and attach to frame
with #6 x 3/4" screws.

Gloria

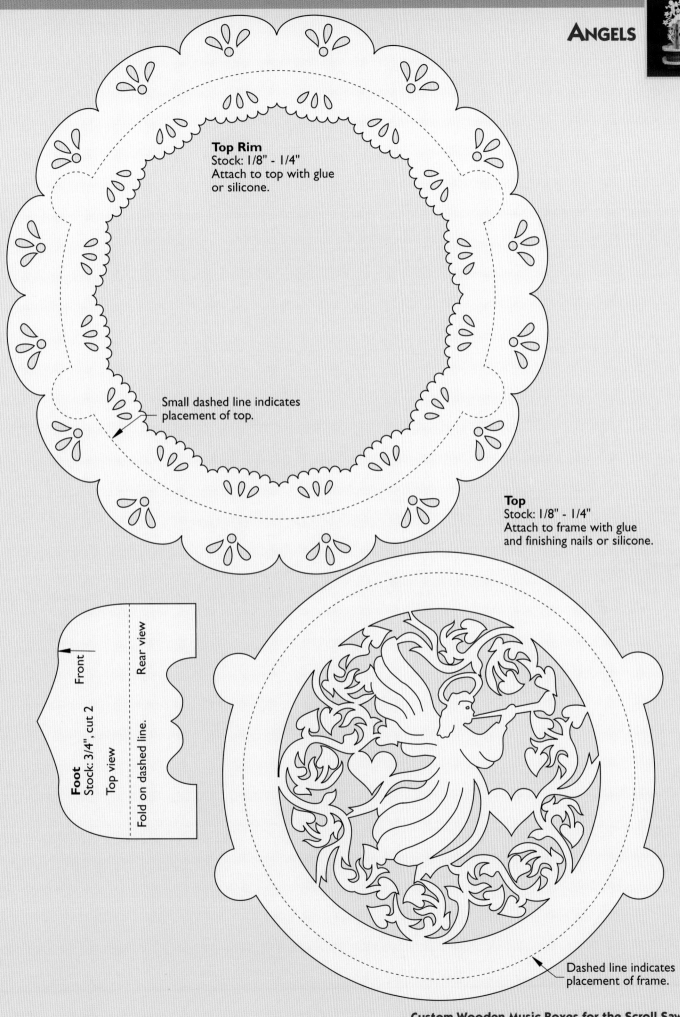

Top Rim
Stock: 1/8" - 1/4"
Attach to top with glue
or silicone.

Small dashed line indicates
placement of top.

Top
Stock: 1/8" - 1/4"
Attach to frame with glue
and finishing nails or silicone.

Foot
Stock: 3/4", cut 2

Front

Rear view

Top view

Fold on dashed line.

Dashed line indicates
placement of frame.

Gloria

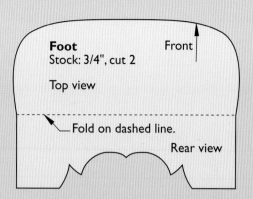

Foot
Stock: 3/4", cut 2

Front

Top view

Fold on dashed line.

Rear view

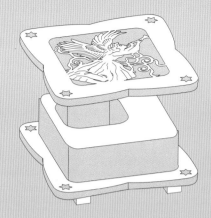

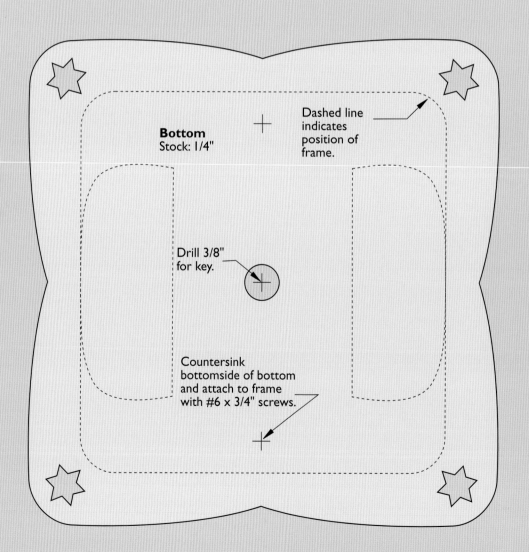

Bottom
Stock: 1/4"

Dashed line indicates position of frame.

Drill 3/8" for key.

Countersink bottomside of bottom and attach to frame with #6 x 3/4" screws.

Celestial Song

Top
Stock: 1/4"

Frame
Stock: 1 1/2"

Circle indicates
position of key and
turntable shafts.

Cut out for music box

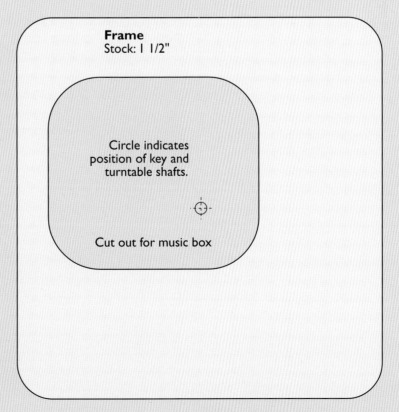

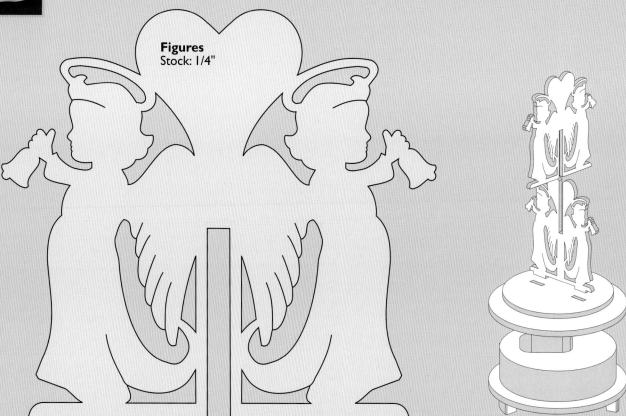

Figures
Stock: 1/4"

Turntable
Stock: 1/4"
Countersink the bottomside
with a 1" Forstner bit 1/16"
deep. Secure the metal turntable
with glue or silicone.

Dashed line
indicates position
of metal turntable
on bottomside.

Adjust slots, if
necessary, for
thickness of
material used.

Roundover top
edge by sanding.

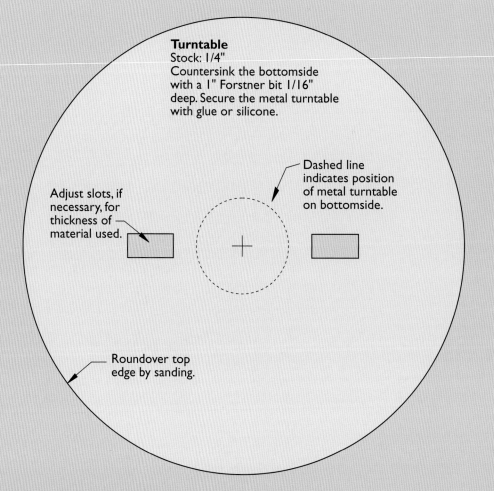

Cherubs

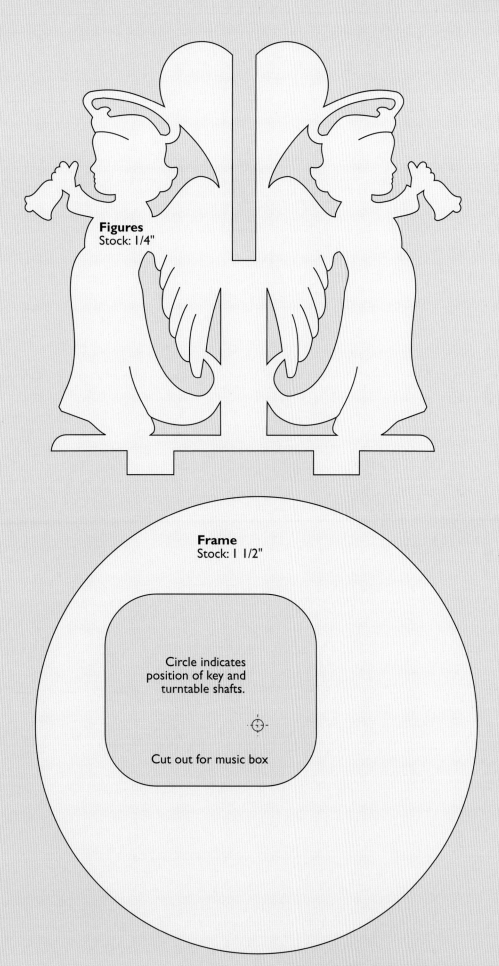

Figures
Stock: 1/4"

Frame
Stock: 1 1/2"

Circle indicates
position of key and
turntable shafts.

Cut out for music box

Cherubs

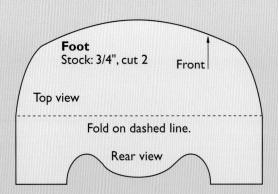

Foot
Stock: 3/4", cut 2

Front

Top view

- - - - - - - - - - - - -

Fold on dashed line.

Rear view

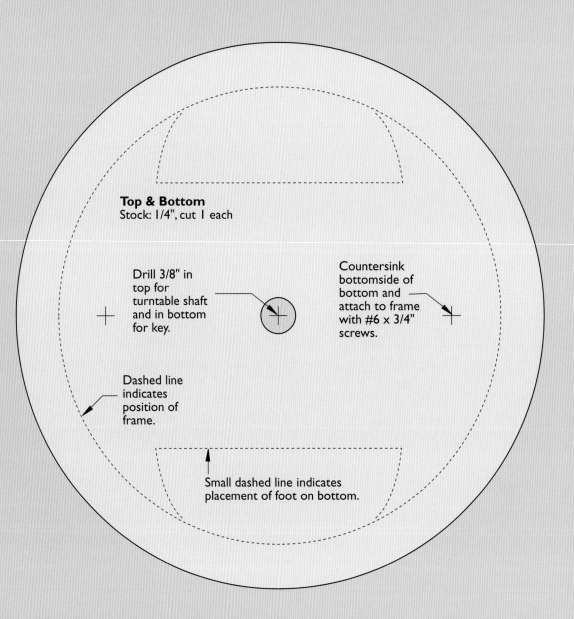

Top & Bottom
Stock: 1/4", cut 1 each

Drill 3/8" in top for turntable shaft and in bottom for key.

Countersink bottomside of bottom and attach to frame with #6 x 3/4" screws.

Dashed line indicates position of frame.

Small dashed line indicates placement of foot on bottom.

ANGELS

Cherubs

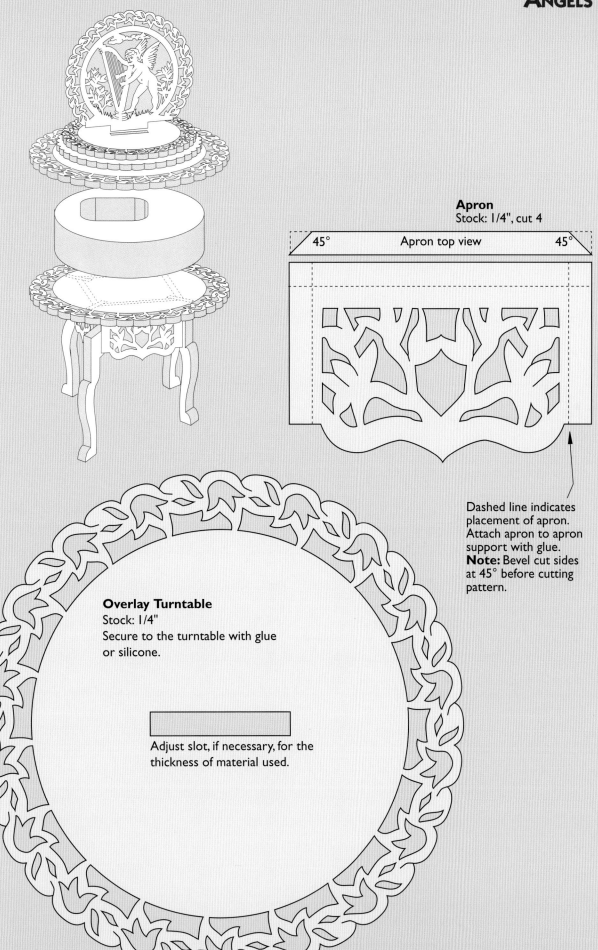

Apron
Stock: 1/4", cut 4

| 45° | Apron top view | 45° |

Dashed line indicates placement of apron. Attach apron to apron support with glue. **Note:** Bevel cut sides at 45° before cutting pattern.

Realms of Glory

Overlay Turntable
Stock: 1/4"
Secure to the turntable with glue or silicone.

Adjust slot, if necessary, for the thickness of material used.

Frame
Stock: 1 1/2"

Circle indicates
position of key and
turntable shafts.

Cut out for music box

Figure
Stock: 1/4"

Realms of Glory

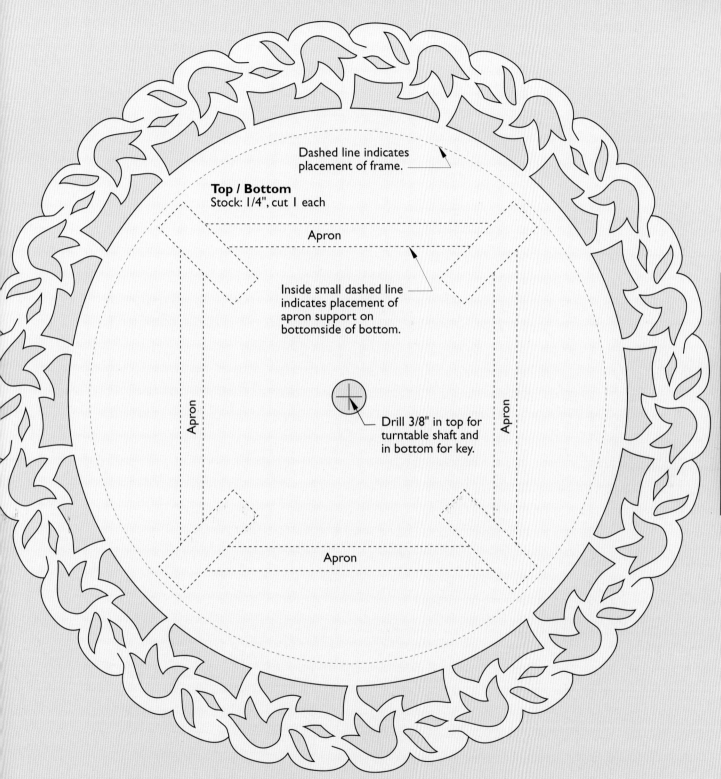

Dashed line indicates placement of frame.

Top / Bottom
Stock: 1/4", cut 1 each

Apron

Inside small dashed line indicates placement of apron support on bottomside of bottom.

Apron

Apron

Drill 3/8" in top for turntable shaft and in bottom for key.

Apron

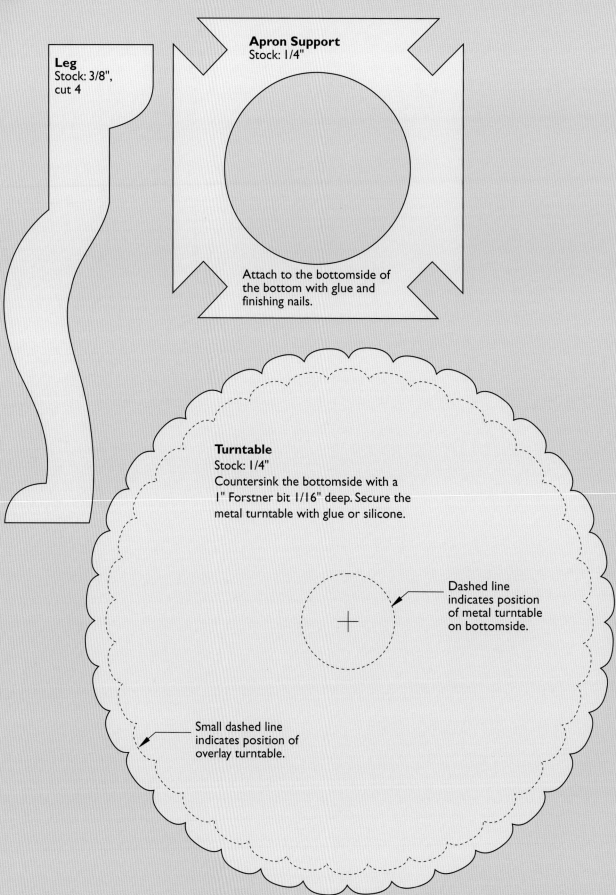

Leg
Stock: 3/8",
cut 4

Apron Support
Stock: 1/4"

Attach to the bottomside of
the bottom with glue and
finishing nails.

Turntable
Stock: 1/4"
Countersink the bottomside with a
1" Forstner bit 1/16" deep. Secure the
metal turntable with glue or silicone.

Dashed line
indicates position
of metal turntable
on bottomside.

Small dashed line
indicates position of
overlay turntable.

Realms of Glory

CHILDREN

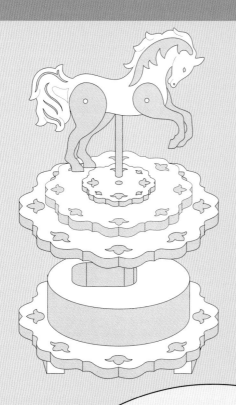

Drill 1/4" hole for dowel.

Turntable Overlay
Stock: 1/4"
Attach to turntable
with glue or silicone.

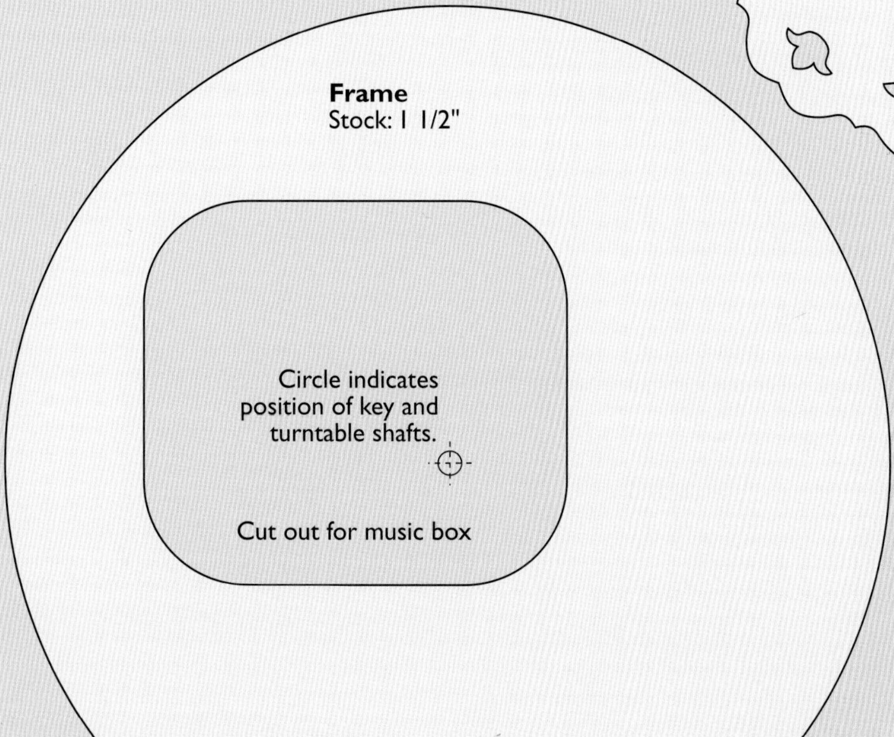

Frame
Stock: 1 1/2"

Circle indicates
position of key and
turntable shafts.

Cut out for music box

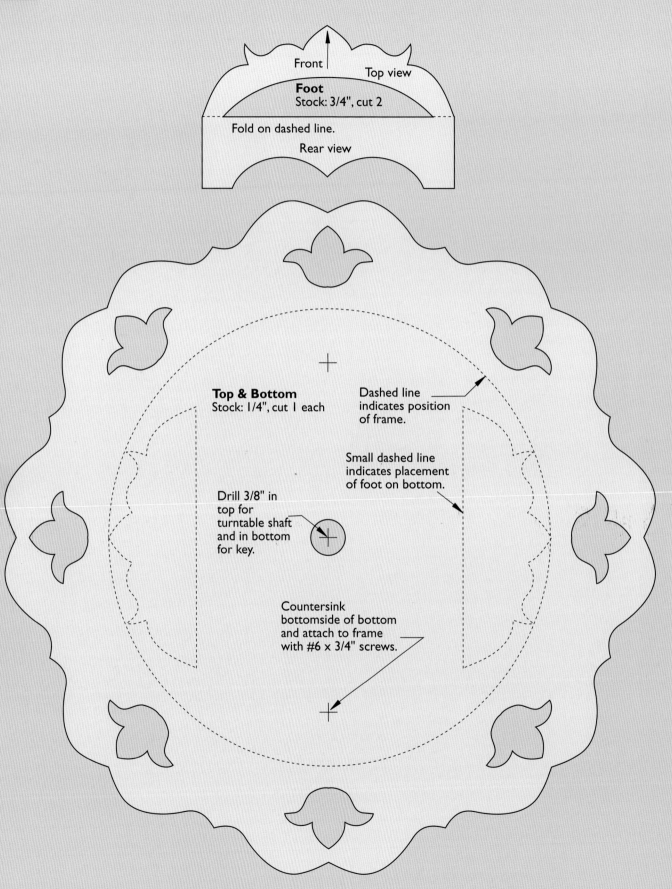

Front

Top view

Foot
Stock: 3/4", cut 2

Fold on dashed line.

Rear view

Top & Bottom
Stock: 1/4", cut 1 each

Dashed line indicates position of frame.

Small dashed line indicates placement of foot on bottom.

Drill 3/8" in top for turntable shaft and in bottom for key.

Countersink bottomside of bottom and attach to frame with #6 x 3/4" screws.

Prancing Pony

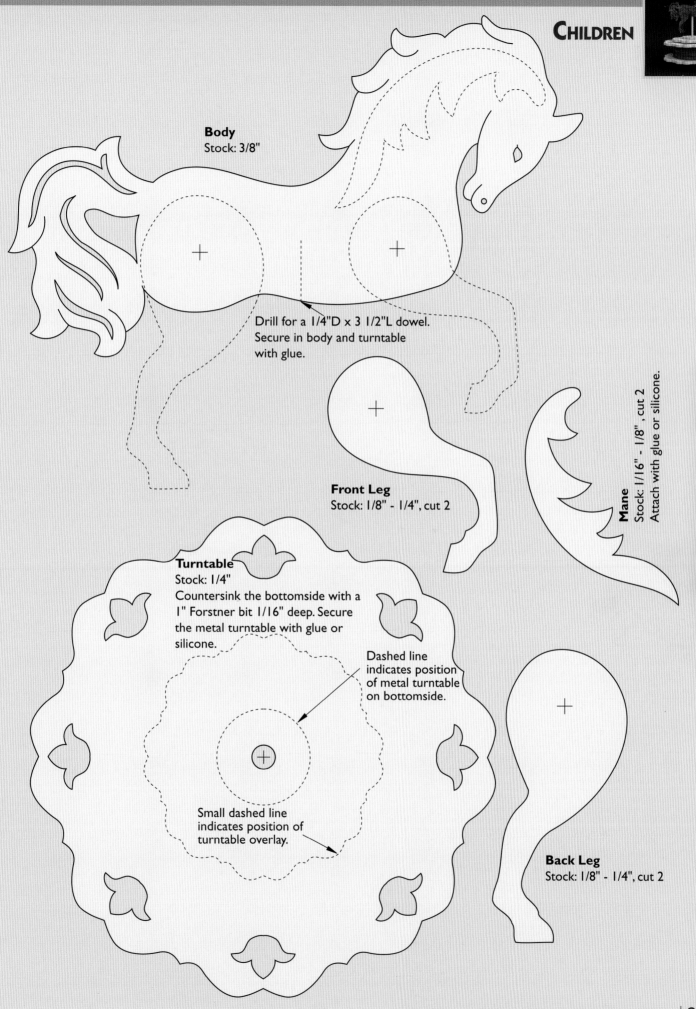

Body
Stock: 3/8"

Drill for a 1/4"D x 3 1/2"L dowel. Secure in body and turntable with glue.

Front Leg
Stock: 1/8" - 1/4", cut 2

Mane
Stock: 1/16" - 1/8", cut 2
Attach with glue or silicone.

Prancing Pony

Turntable
Stock: 1/4"
Countersink the bottomside with a 1" Forstner bit 1/16" deep. Secure the metal turntable with glue or silicone.

Dashed line indicates position of metal turntable on bottomside.

Small dashed line indicates position of turntable overlay.

Back Leg
Stock: 1/8" - 1/4", cut 2

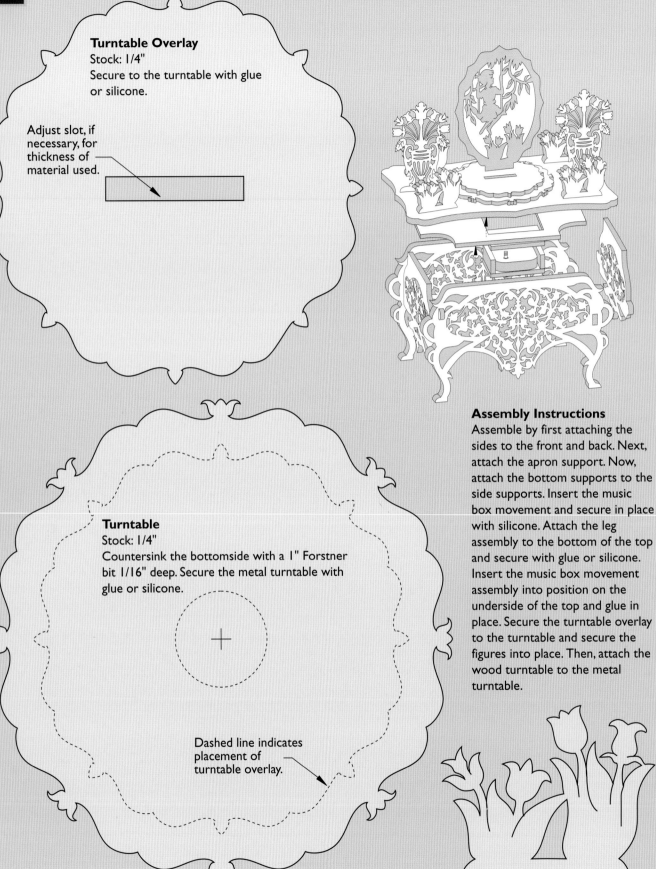

Turntable Overlay
Stock: 1/4"
Secure to the turntable with glue or silicone.

Adjust slot, if necessary, for thickness of material used.

Turntable
Stock: 1/4"
Countersink the bottomside with a 1" Forstner bit 1/16" deep. Secure the metal turntable with glue or silicone.

Dashed line indicates placement of turntable overlay.

Assembly Instructions
Assemble by first attaching the sides to the front and back. Next, attach the apron support. Now, attach the bottom supports to the side supports. Insert the music box movement and secure in place with silicone. Attach the leg assembly to the bottom of the top and secure with glue or silicone. Insert the music box movement assembly into position on the underside of the top and glue in place. Secure the turntable overlay to the turntable and secure the figures into place. Then, attach the wood turntable to the metal turntable.

Corner Tulips
Stock: 3/8", cut 4
Secure to top with glue or silicone.

Tulips

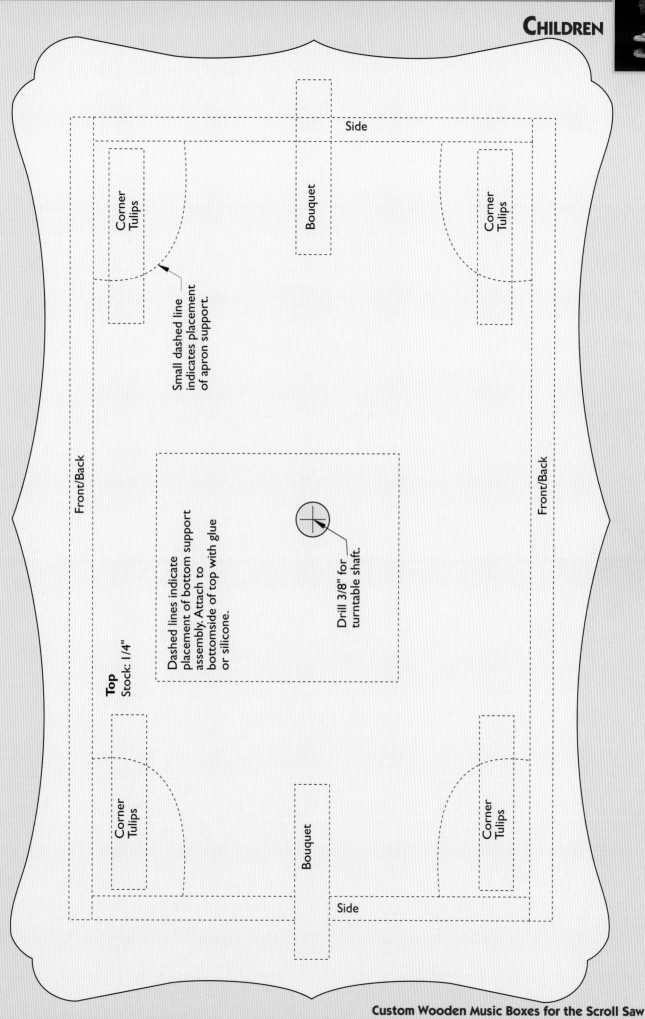

Side

Corner Tulips

Bouquet

Corner Tulips

Small dashed line indicates placement of apron support.

Front/Back

Top
Stock: 1/4"

Front/Back

Dashed lines indicate placement of bottom support assembly. Attach to bottomside of top with glue or silicone.

Drill 3/8" for turntable shaft.

Corner Tulips

Bouquet

Corner Tulips

Side

Tulips

Attach apron support with
glue and finishing nails.

Front & Back
Stock: 1/4", cut 1 each

Bouquet
Stock: 3/8", cut 2

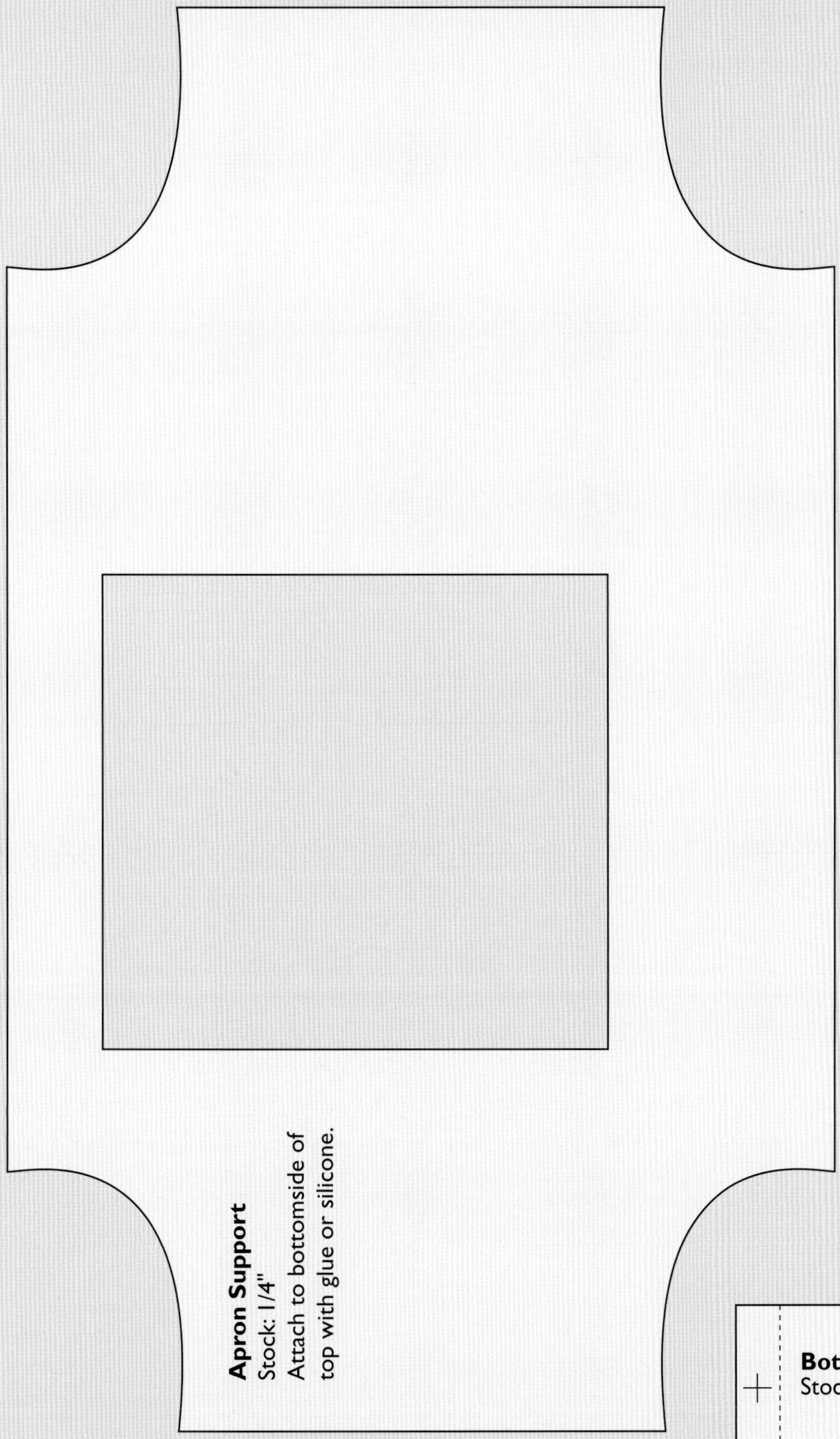

Tulips

Apron Support
Stock: 1/4"
Attach to bottomside of
top with glue or silicone.

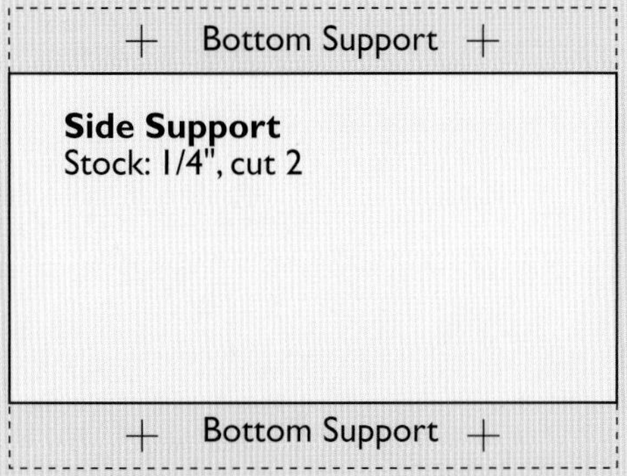

+ Bottom Support +

Side Support
Stock: 1/4", cut 2

+ Bottom Support +

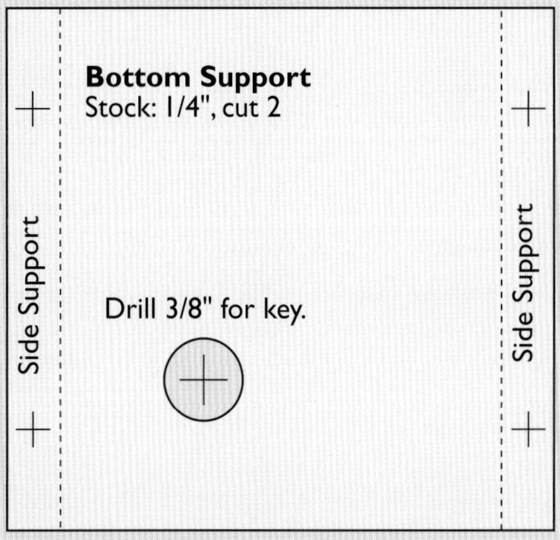

Bottom Support
Stock: 1/4", cut 2

Side Support

Side Support

Drill 3/8" for key.

Side
Stock: 1/4", cut 2

Figure
Stock: 1/4"

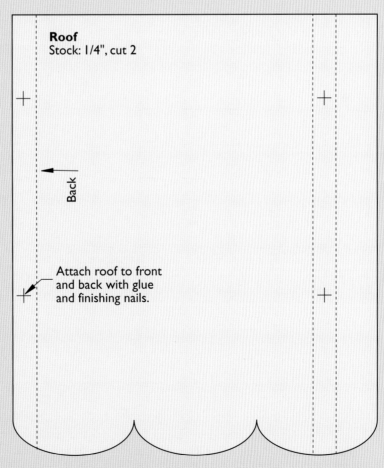

Roof
Stock: 1/4", cut 2

Back

Attach roof to front
and back with glue
and finishing nails.

Attach crest to front edge of roof with glue and finishing nails.

Crest
Stock: 1/4"

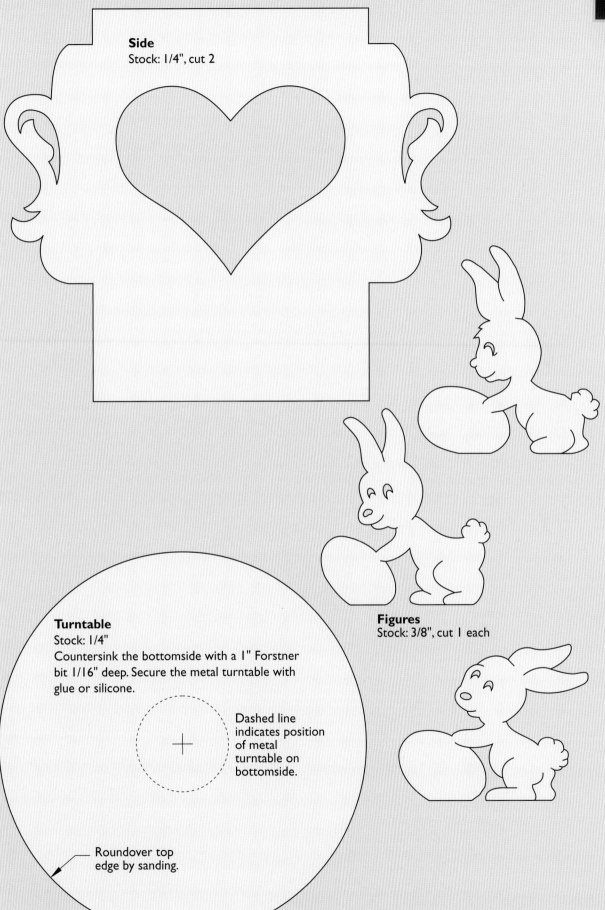

Side
Stock: 1/4", cut 2

Bunny Trail

Figures
Stock: 3/8", cut 1 each

Turntable
Stock: 1/4"
Countersink the bottomside with a 1" Forstner bit 1/16" deep. Secure the metal turntable with glue or silicone.

Dashed line indicates position of metal turntable on bottomside.

Roundover top edge by sanding.

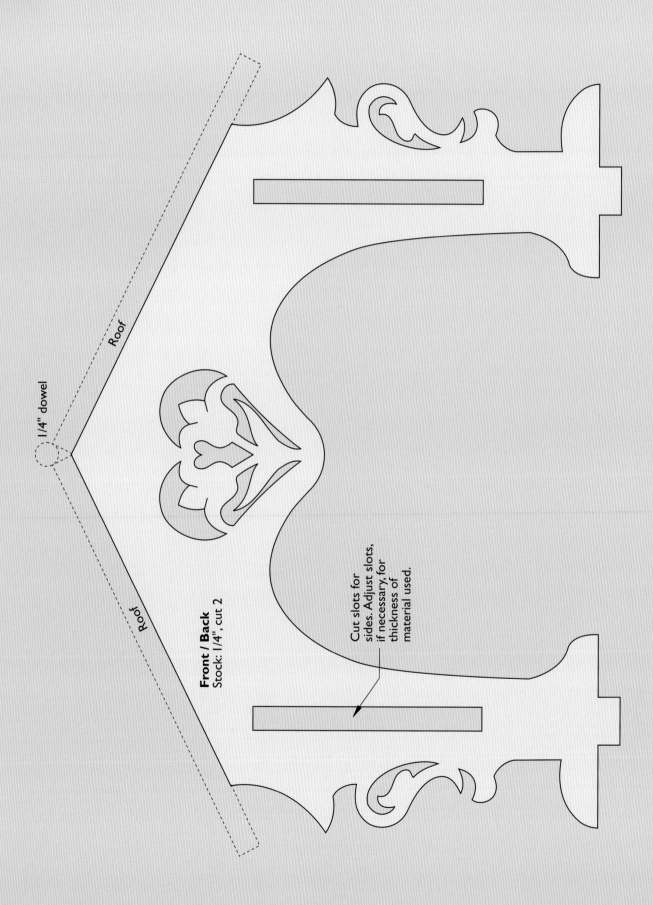

Roof

1/4" dowel

Roof

Front / Back
Stock: 1/4", cut 2

Cut slots for
sides. Adjust slots,
if necessary, for
thickness of
material used.

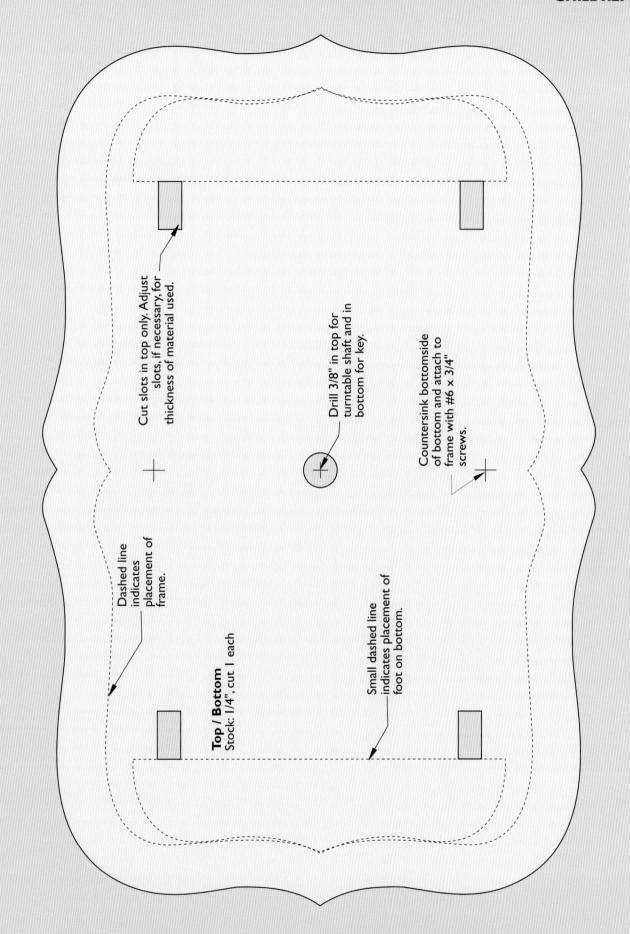

Cut slots in top only. Adjust slots, if necessary, for thickness of material used.

Drill 3/8" in top for turntable shaft and in bottom for key.

Countersink bottomside of bottom and attach to frame with #6 x 3/4" screws.

Dashed line indicates placement of frame.

Top / Bottom
Stock: 1/4", cut 1 each

Small dashed line indicates placement of foot on bottom.

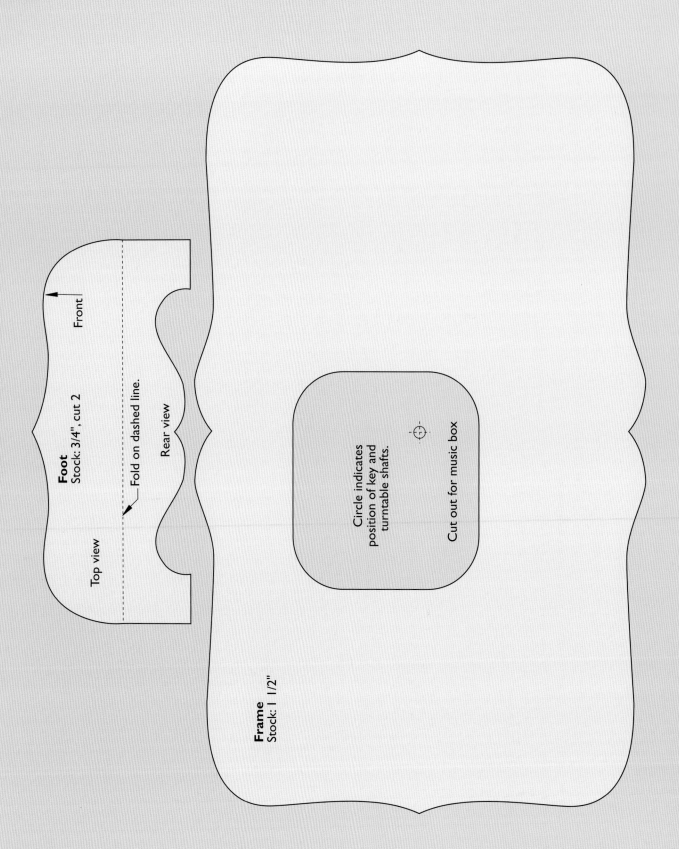

Foot
Stock: 3/4", cut 2

Front

Fold on dashed line.

Rear view

Top view

Frame
Stock: 1 1/2"

Circle indicates
position of key and
turntable shafts.

Cut out for music box

CHRISTMAS

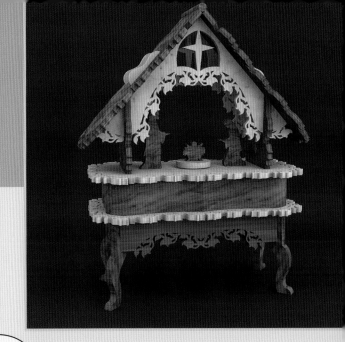

Roof
Stock: 1/4", cut 2

Cut slots to attach to arches. Adjust slots, if necessary, for thickness of material used.

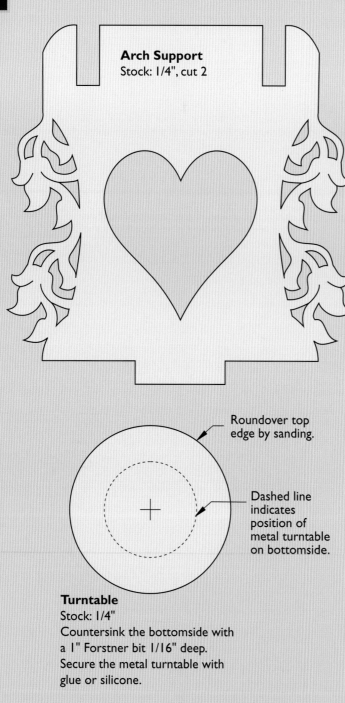

Arch Support
Stock: 1/4", cut 2

Roundover top
edge by sanding.

Dashed line
indicates
position of
metal turntable
on bottomside.

Turntable
Stock: 1/4"
Countersink the bottomside with
a 1" Forstner bit 1/16" deep.
Secure the metal turntable with
glue or silicone.

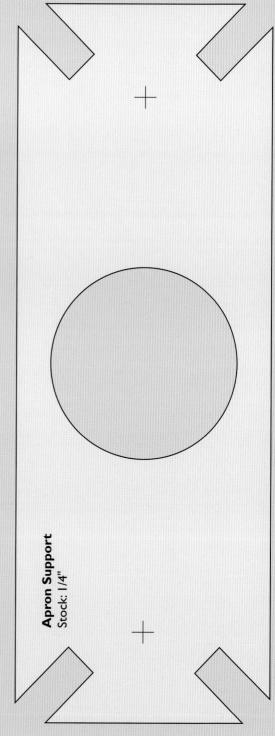

Apron Support
Stock: 1/4"

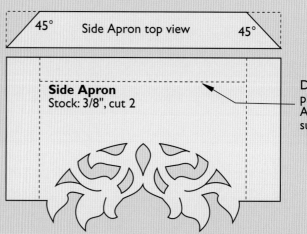

45° Side Apron top view 45°

Side Apron
Stock: 3/8", cut 2

Dashed line indic
placement of apr
Attach apron to
support with glue

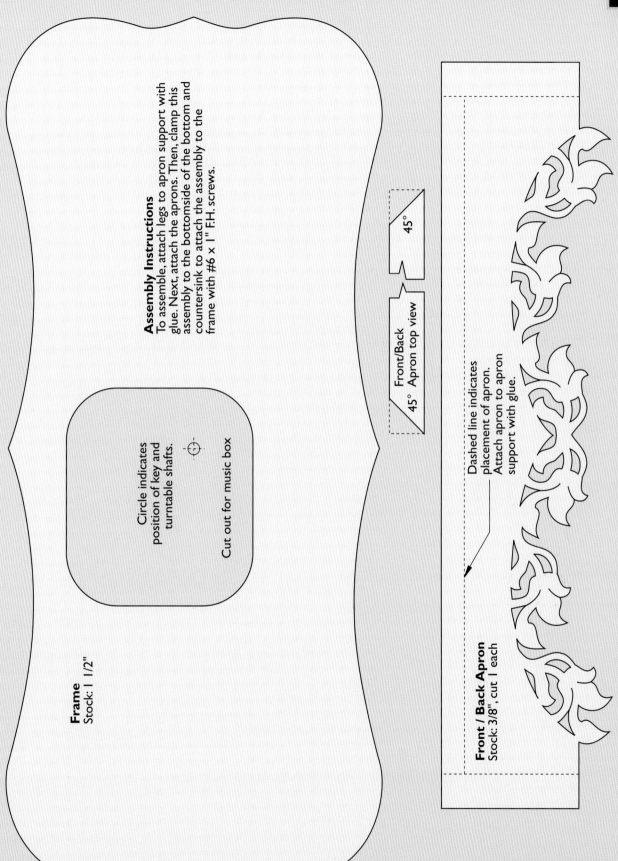

Assembly Instructions

To assemble, attach legs to apron support with glue. Next, attach the aprons. Then, clamp this assembly to the bottomside of the bottom and countersink to attach the assembly to the frame with #6 x 1" F.H. screws.

Circle indicates position of key and turntable shafts.

Cut out for music box

Frame
Stock: 1 1/2"

Front/Back
45° Apron top view

45°

Dashed line indicates placement of apron. Attach apron to apron support with glue.

Front / Back Apron
Stock: 3/8", cut 1 each

Holy Night

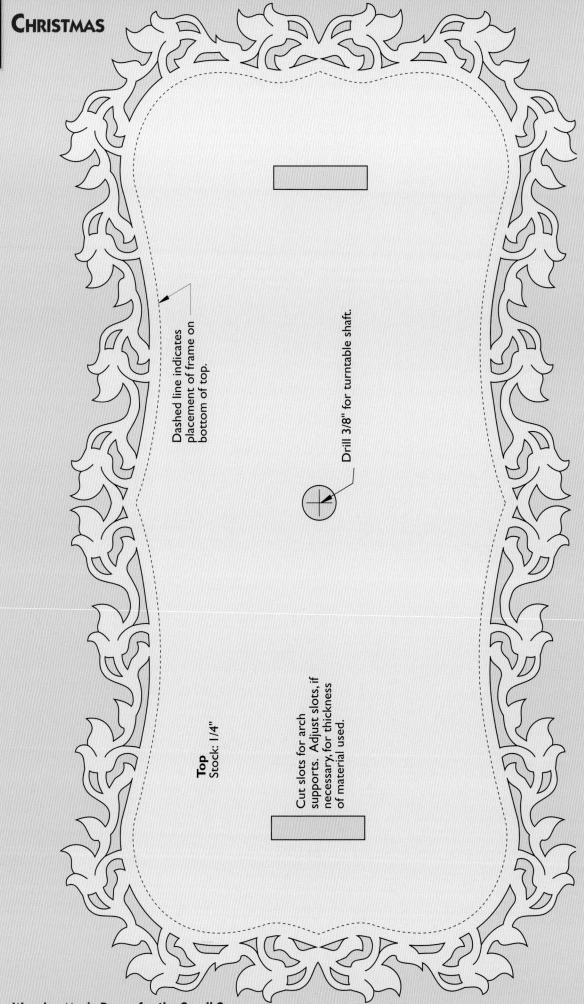

Dashed line indicates placement of frame on bottom of top.

Drill 3/8" for turntable shaft.

Top
Stock: 1/4"

Cut slots for arch supports. Adjust slots, if necessary, for thickness of material used.

Leg

Side Apron

Leg

Drill 3/8" for key.

Inside small dashed line indicates placement of apron support.

Bottom
Stock: 1/4"

Front/Back Apron

Dashed line indicates placement of frame on top of bottom.

Front/Back Apron

Leg

Leg

Side Apron

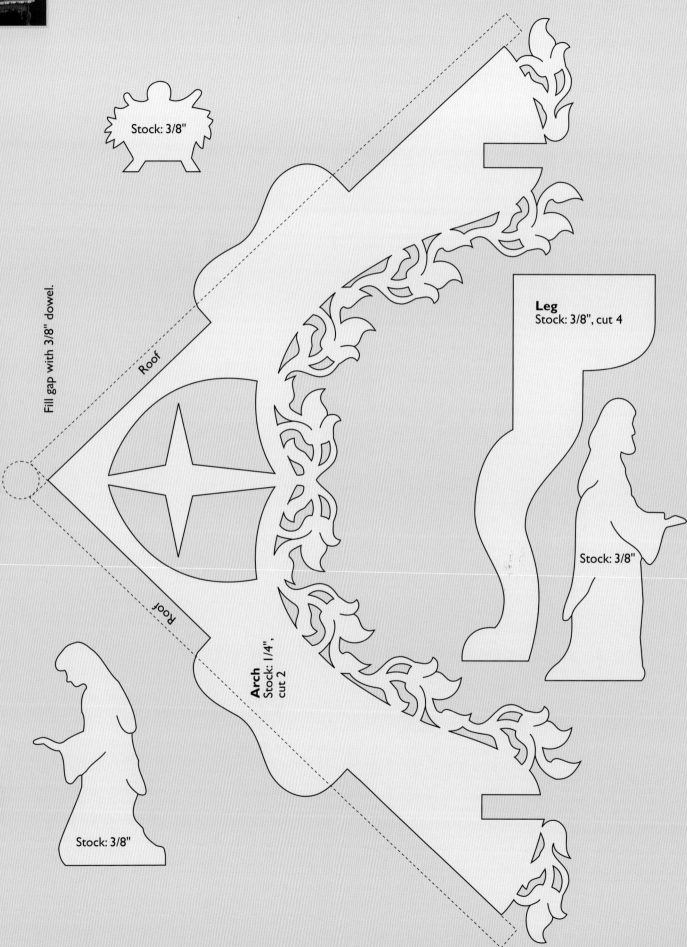

Stock: 3/8"

Fill gap with 3/8" dowel.

Roof

Roof

Arch
Stock: 1/4",
cut 2

Leg
Stock: 3/8", cut 4

Stock: 3/8"

Stock: 3/8"

Front view

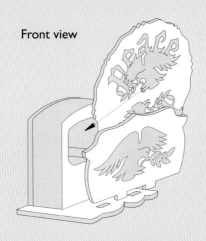

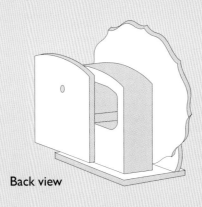

Back view

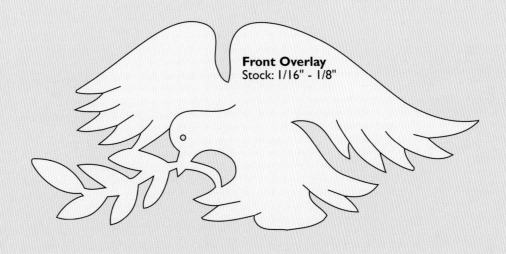

Front Overlay
Stock: 1/16" - 1/8"

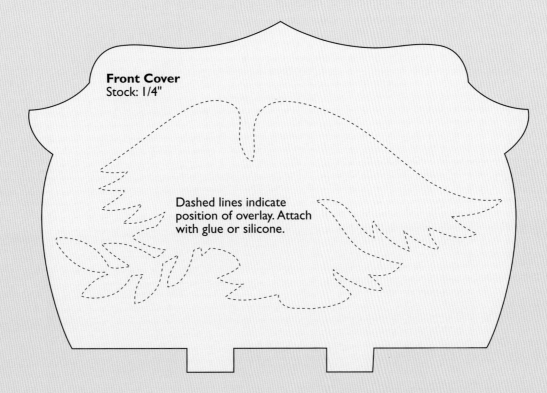

Front Cover
Stock: 1/4"

Dashed lines indicate
position of overlay. Attach
with glue or silicone.

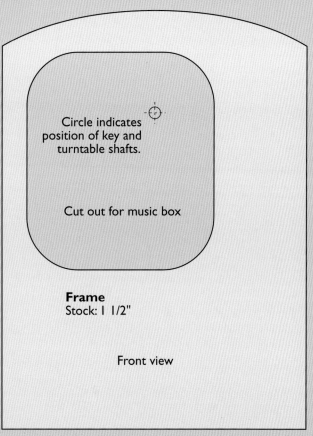

Circle indicates position of key and turntable shafts.

Cut out for music box

Frame
Stock: 1 1/2"

Front view

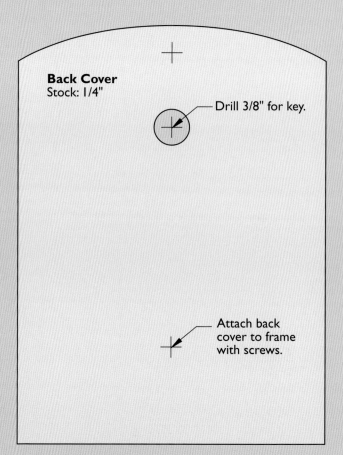

Back Cover
Stock: 1/4"

Drill 3/8" for key.

Attach back cover to frame with screws.

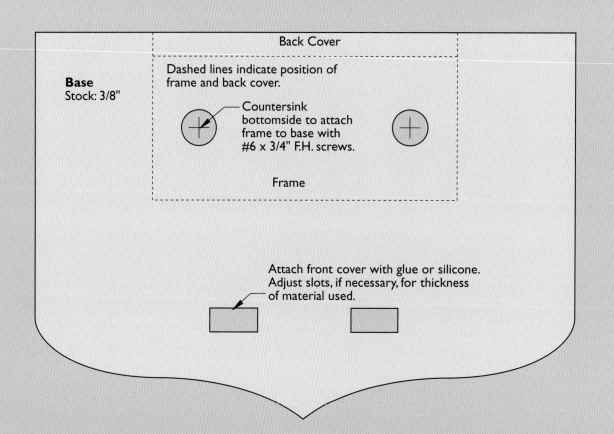

Back Cover

Base
Stock: 3/8"

Dashed lines indicate position of frame and back cover.

Countersink bottomside to attach frame to base with #6 x 3/4" F.H. screws.

Frame

Attach front cover with glue or silicone. Adjust slots, if necessary, for thickness of material used.

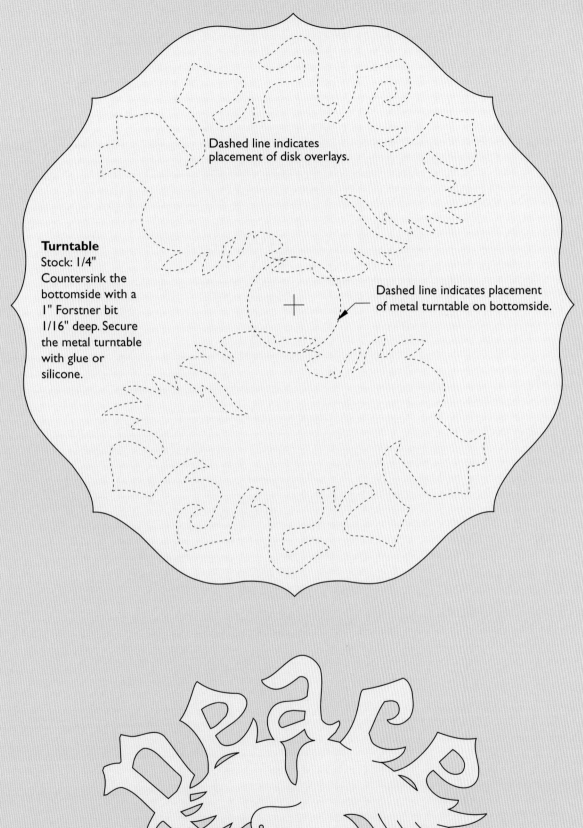

Dashed line indicates placement of disk overlays.

Dashed line indicates placement of metal turntable on bottomside.

Turntable
Stock: 1/4"
Countersink the bottomside with a 1" Forstner bit 1/16" deep. Secure the metal turntable with glue or silicone.

Disk Overlay
Stock: 1/16" - 1/8", cut 2

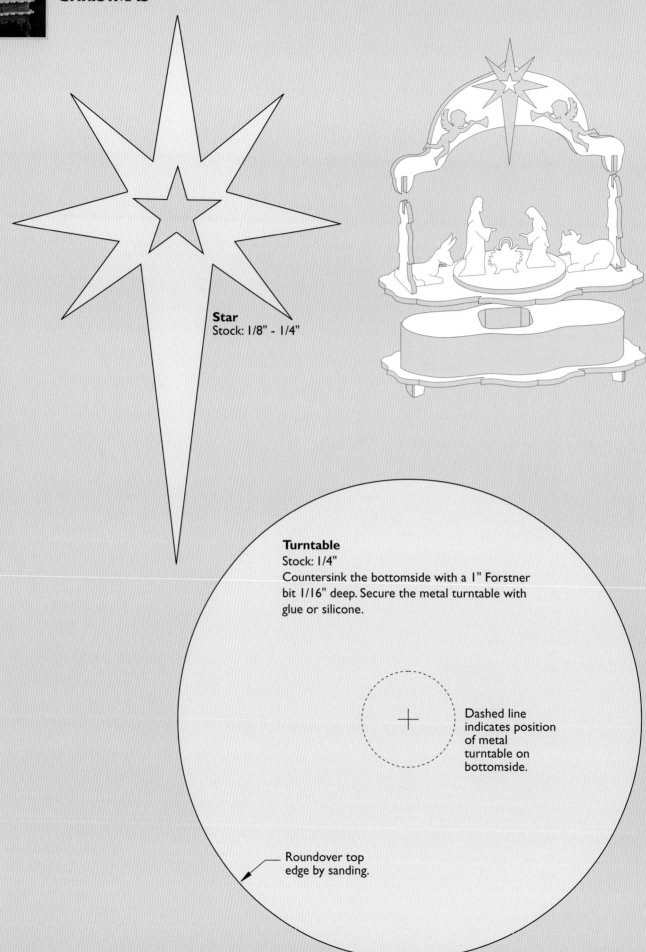

Star
Stock: 1/8" - 1/4"

Turntable
Stock: 1/4"
Countersink the bottomside with a 1" Forstner bit 1/16" deep. Secure the metal turntable with glue or silicone.

Dashed line indicates position of metal turntable on bottomside.

Roundover top edge by sanding.

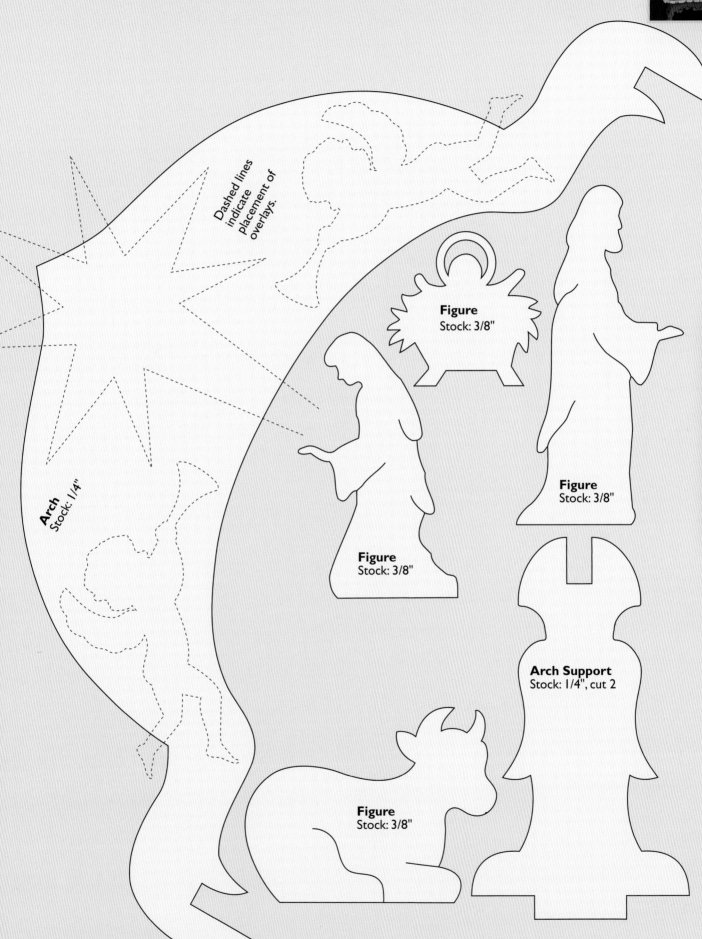

Dashed lines indicate placement of overlays.

Arch
Stock: 1/4"

Figure
Stock: 3/8"

Figure
Stock: 3/8"

Figure
Stock: 3/8"

Figure
Stock: 3/8"

Arch Support
Stock: 1/4", cut 2

Figure
Stock: 3/8"

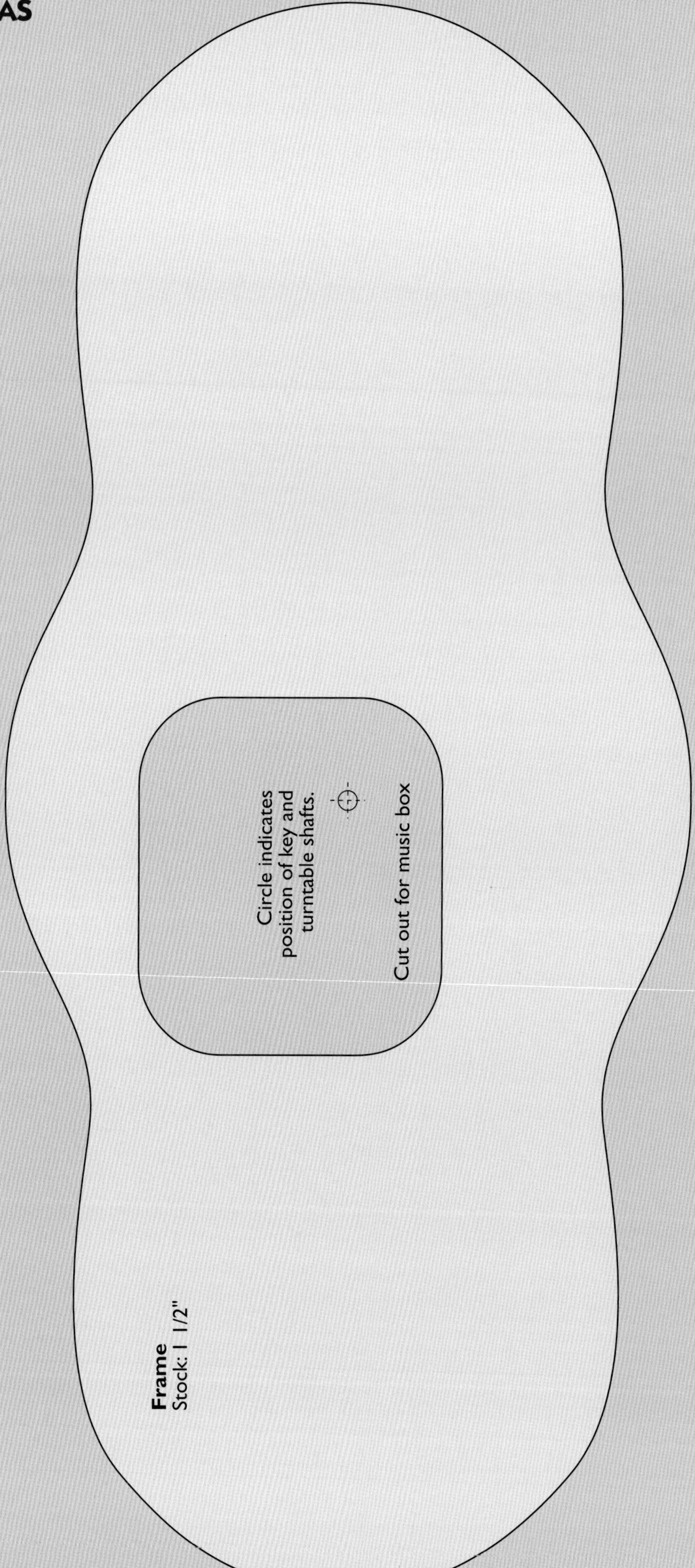

CHRISTMAS

Circle indicates
position of key and
turntable shafts.

Cut out for music box

Frame
Stock: 1 1/2"

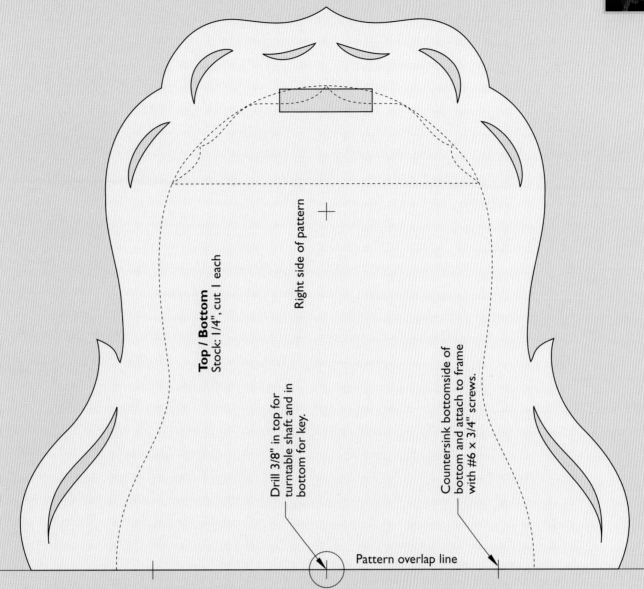

Right side of pattern

Top / Bottom
Stock: 1/4", cut 1 each

Drill 3/8" in top for
turntable shaft and in
bottom for key.

Countersink bottomside of
bottom and attach to frame
with #6 x 3/4" screws.

Pattern overlap line

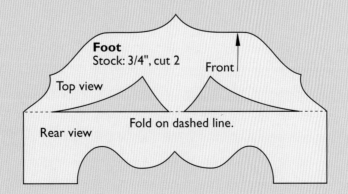

Foot
Stock: 3/4", cut 2

Top view

Front

Rear view

Fold on dashed line.

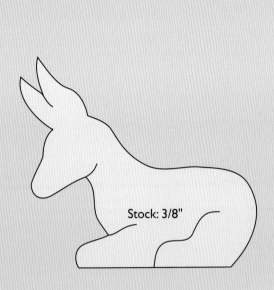

Stock: 3/8"

Angel
Stock: 1/16" - 1/8",
cut 2

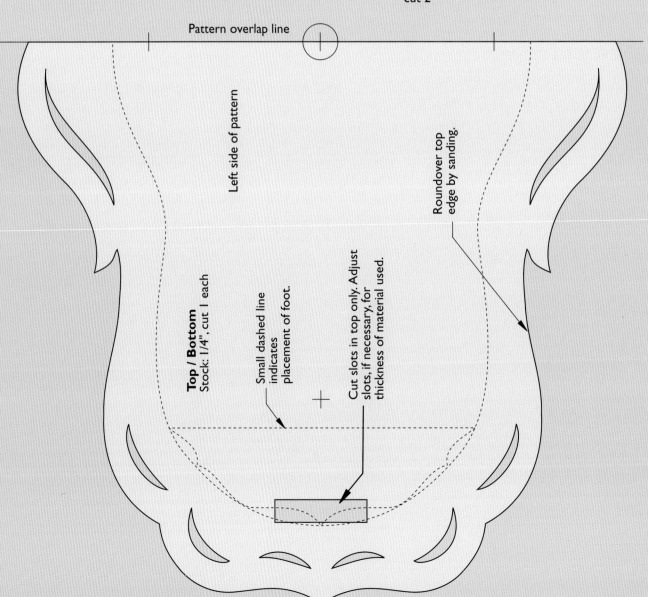

Pattern overlap line

Left side of pattern

Roundover top
edge by sanding.

Top / Bottom
Stock: 1/4", cut 1 each

Small dashed line
indicates
placement of foot.

Cut slots in top only. Adjust
slots, if necessary, for
thickness of material used.

Back Cover
Stock: 1/4"

Drill 3/8" for key.

Attach back
cover to frame
with screws.

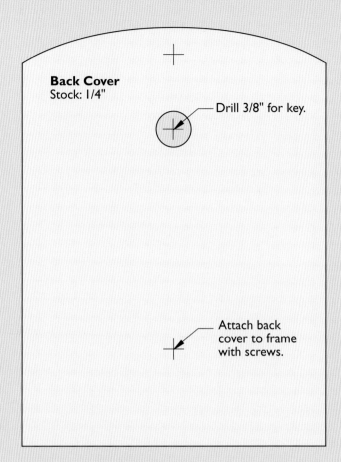

Front view

Back view

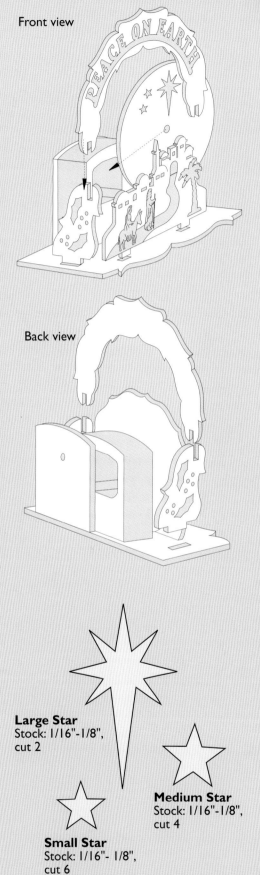

Cut out for music box

Circle indicates
position of key and
turntable shafts.

Frame
Stock: 1 1/2"

Front view

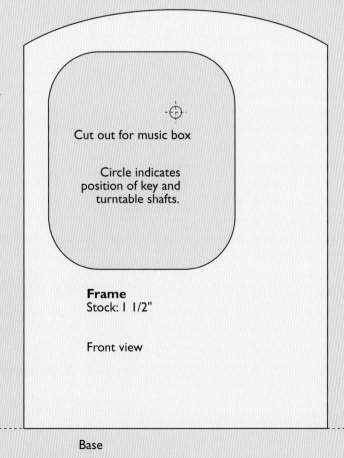

Large Star
Stock: 1/16"-1/8",
cut 2

Medium Star
Stock: 1/16"-1/8",
cut 4

Small Star
Stock: 1/16"- 1/8",
cut 6

Base

Peace on Earth

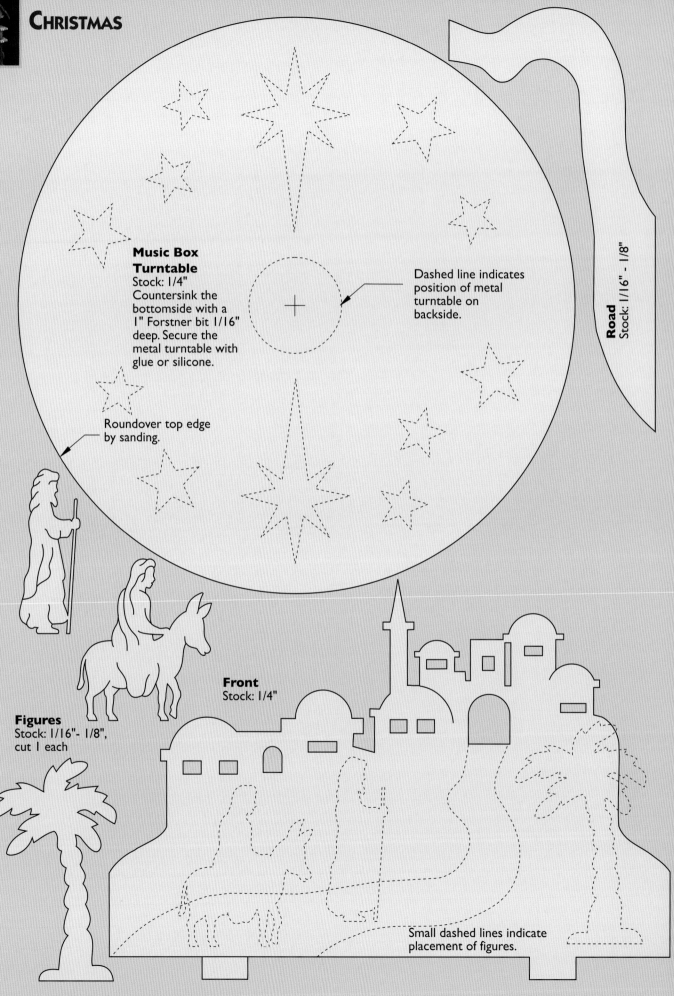

Music Box Turntable
Stock: 1/4"
Countersink the bottomside with a 1" Forstner bit 1/16" deep. Secure the metal turntable with glue or silicone.

Dashed line indicates position of metal turntable on backside.

Roundover top edge by sanding.

Road
Stock: 1/16" - 1/8"

Figures
Stock: 1/16"- 1/8", cut 1 each

Front
Stock: 1/4"

Small dashed lines indicate placement of figures.

Dashed line indicates placement of top overlay.

Front

PEACE ON EARTH

PEACE ON EARTH

Arch Support
Stock: 1/4", cut 2

Top Overlay
Stock: 1/16" - 1/8"

Arch
Stock: 1/4"

Peace on Earth

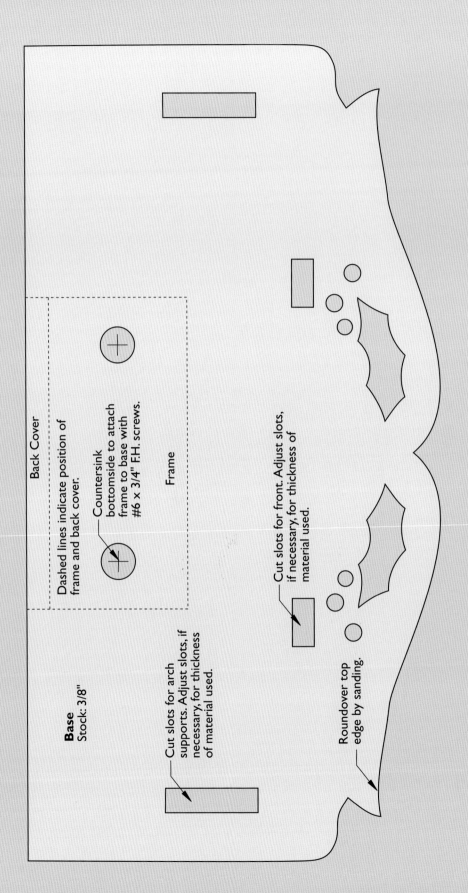

Back Cover

Dashed lines indicate position of
frame and back cover.

Countersink
bottomside to attach
frame to base with
#6 x 3/4" F.H. screws.

Frame

Base
Stock: 3/8"

Cut slots for arch
supports. Adjust slots, if
necessary, for thickness
of material used.

Cut slots for front. Adjust slots,
if necessary, for thickness of
material used.

Roundover top
edge by sanding.

Front view

Circle indicates position of key and turntable shafts.

Cut out for music box

Frame
Stock: 1 1/2"

Front view

Base

Back view

Front
Stock: 1/4"

Dashed lines indicate position of overlay. Attach with glue or silicone.

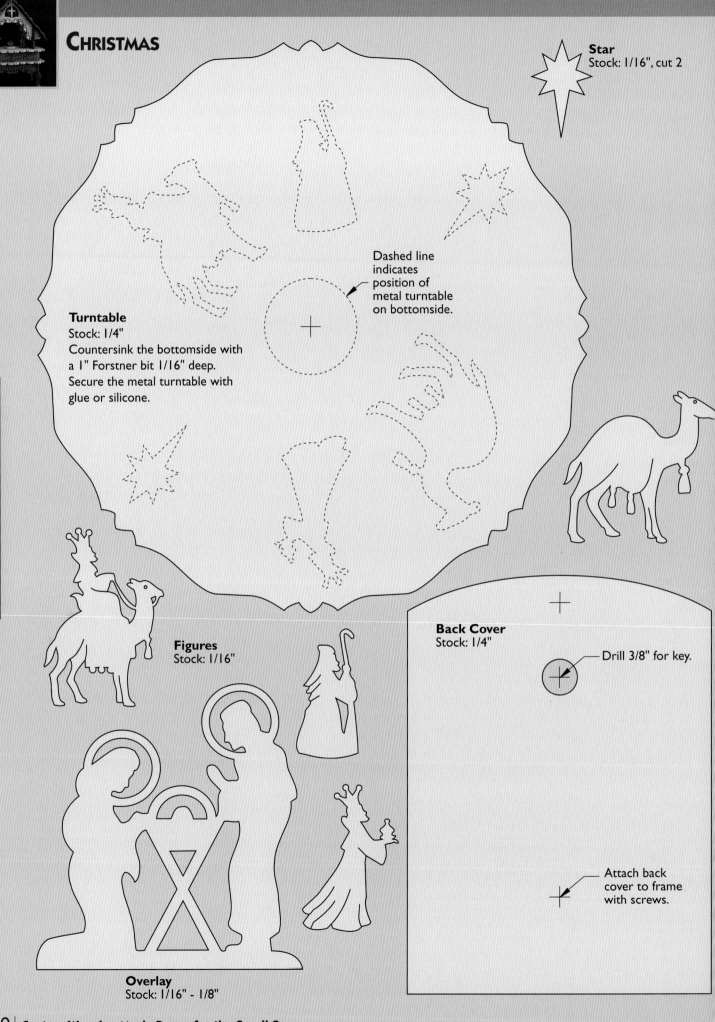

Star
Stock: 1/16", cut 2

Turntable
Stock: 1/4"
Countersink the bottomside with a 1" Forstner bit 1/16" deep. Secure the metal turntable with glue or silicone.

Dashed line indicates position of metal turntable on bottomside.

Figures
Stock: 1/16"

Overlay
Stock: 1/16" - 1/8"

Back Cover
Stock: 1/4"

Drill 3/8" for key.

Attach back cover to frame with screws.

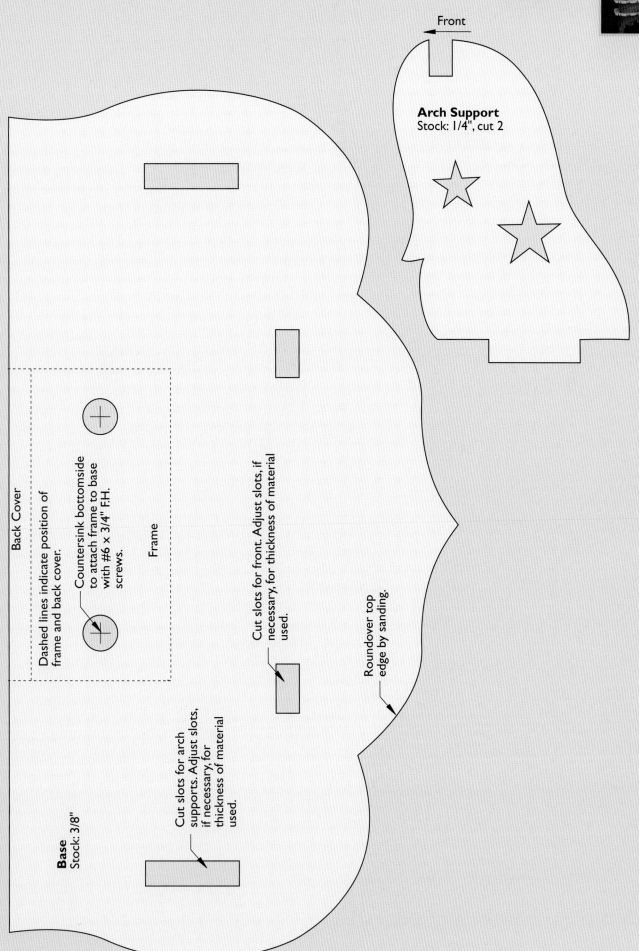

Arch Support
Stock: 1/4", cut 2

Front

Back Cover

Dashed lines indicate position of frame and back cover.

Countersink bottomside to attach frame to base with #6 x 3/4" F.H. screws.

Frame

Cut slots for front. Adjust slots, if necessary, for thickness of material used.

Roundover top edge by sanding.

Cut slots for arch supports. Adjust slots, if necessary, for thickness of material used.

Base
Stock: 3/8"

Away in a Manger

CHRISTMAS

Away in a Manger

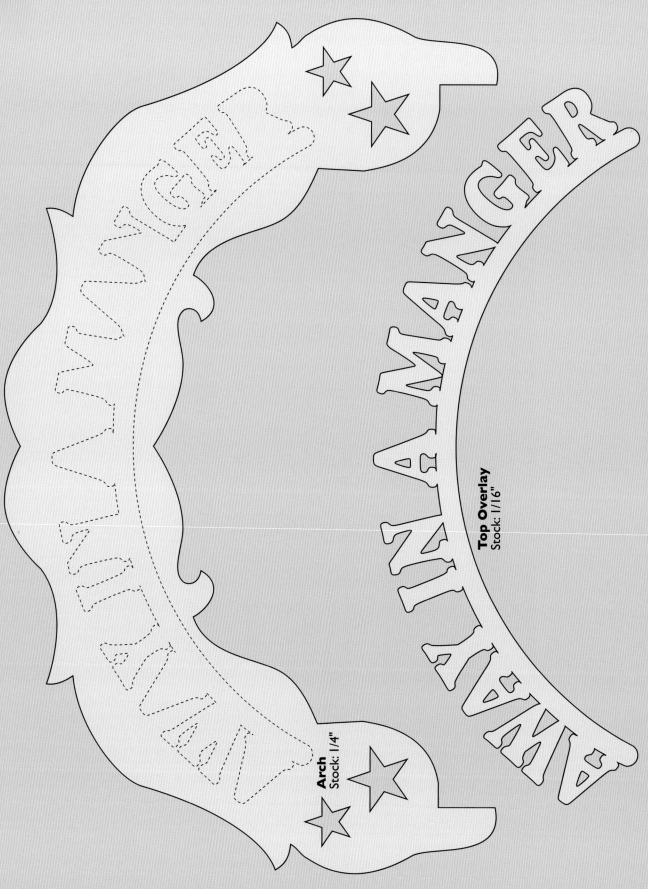

Arch
Stock: 1/4"

Top Overlay
Stock: 1/16"

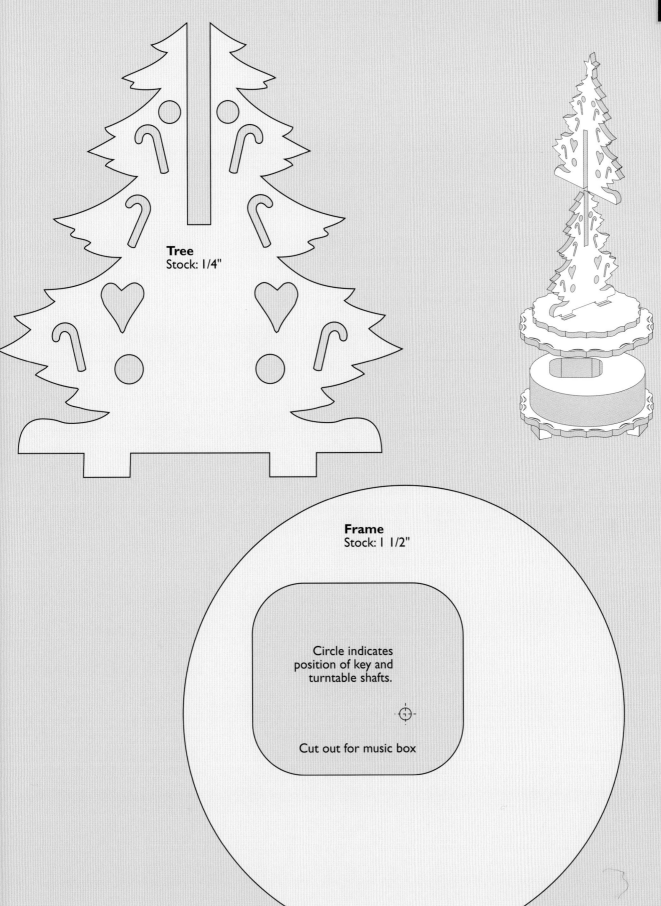

Tree
Stock: 1/4"

Frame
Stock: 1 1/2"

Circle indicates
position of key and
turntable shafts.

Cut out for music box

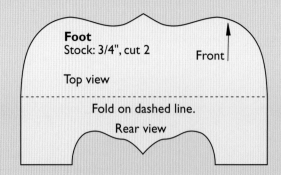

Foot
Stock: 3/4", cut 2

Front

Top view

Fold on dashed line.

Rear view

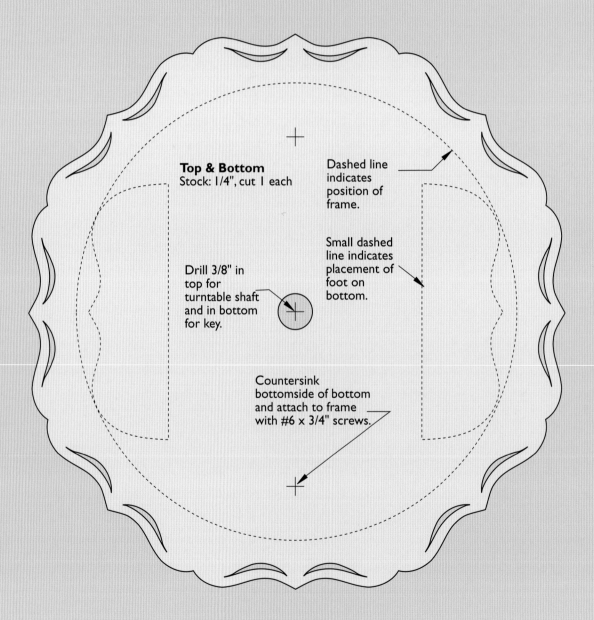

Top & Bottom
Stock: 1/4", cut 1 each

Dashed line indicates position of frame.

Small dashed line indicates placement of foot on bottom.

Drill 3/8" in top for turntable shaft and in bottom for key.

Countersink bottomside of bottom and attach to frame with #6 x 3/4" screws.

Turntable
Stock: 1/4"
Countersink the bottomside with
a 1" Forstner bit 1/16" deep.
Secure the metal turntable with
glue or silicone.

Dashed line
indicates position
of metal
turntable on
bottomside.

Adjust slots, if
necessary, for
thickness of
material used.

Roundover top
edge by sanding.

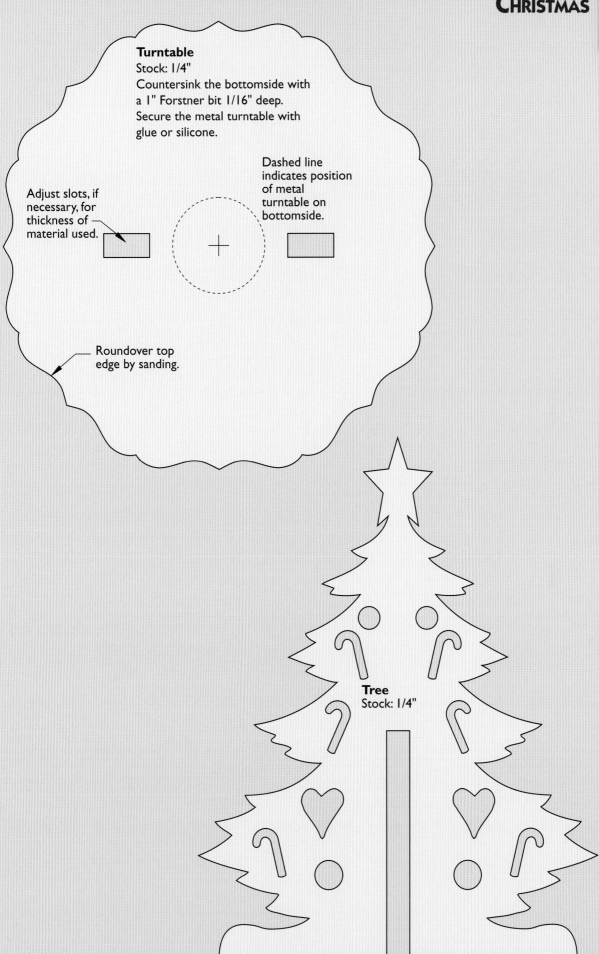

Tree
Stock: 1/4"

O Christmas Tree

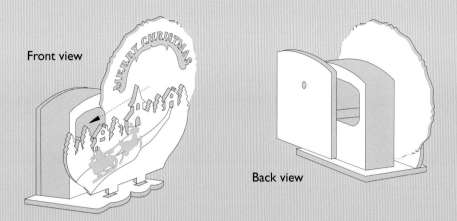

Front view

Back view

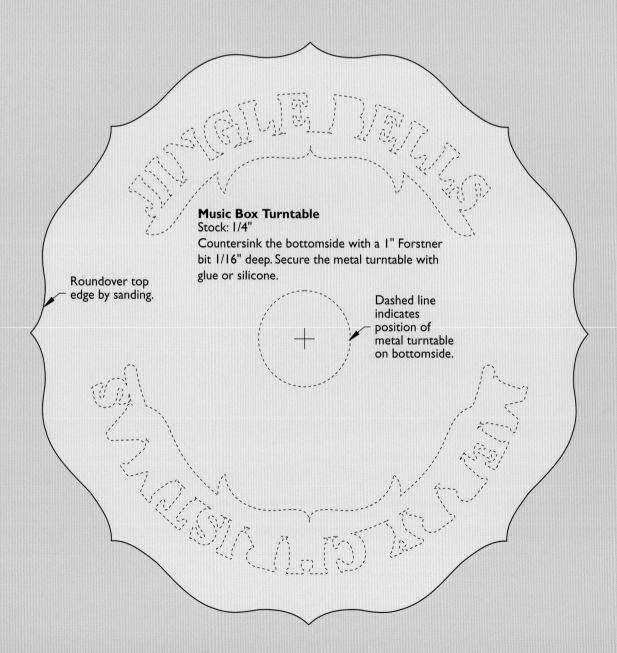

Music Box Turntable
Stock: 1/4"
Countersink the bottomside with a 1" Forstner bit 1/16" deep. Secure the metal turntable with glue or silicone.

Roundover top edge by sanding.

Dashed line indicates position of metal turntable on bottomside.

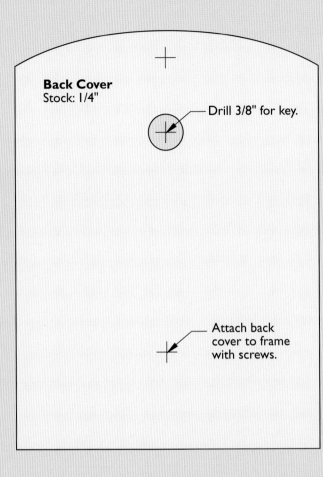

Back Cover
Stock: 1/4"

Drill 3/8" for key.

Attach back
cover to frame
with screws.

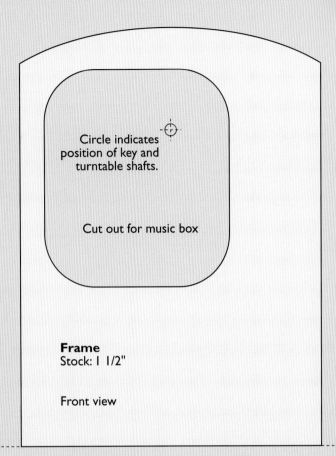

Circle indicates
position of key and
turntable shafts.

Cut out for music box

Frame
Stock: 1 1/2"

Front view

Base

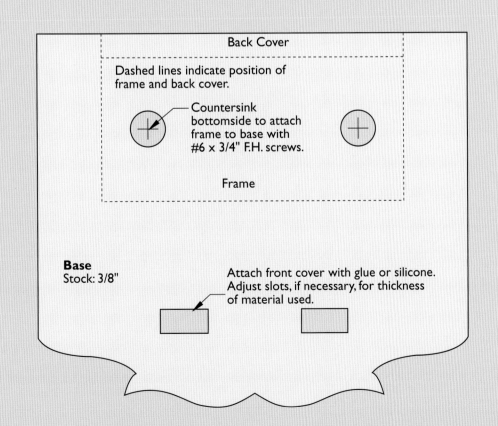

Back Cover

Dashed lines indicate position of
frame and back cover.

Countersink
bottomside to attach
frame to base with
#6 x 3/4" F.H. screws.

Frame

Base
Stock: 3/8"

Attach front cover with glue or silicone.
Adjust slots, if necessary, for thickness
of material used.

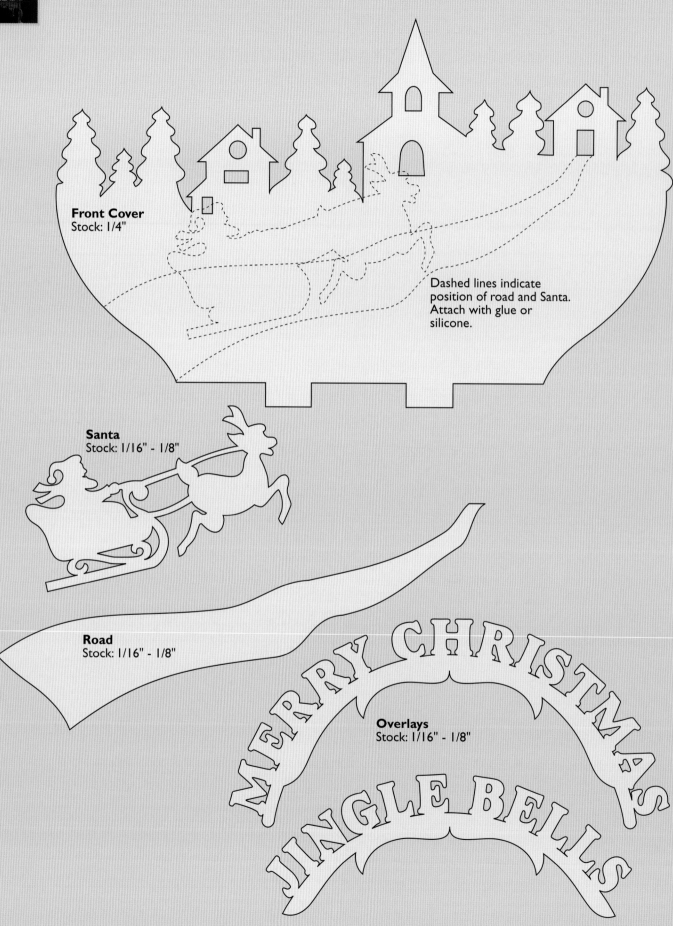

Front Cover
Stock: 1/4"

Dashed lines indicate position of road and Santa. Attach with glue or silicone.

Santa
Stock: 1/16" - 1/8"

Road
Stock: 1/16" - 1/8"

Overlays
Stock: 1/16" - 1/8"

MERRY CHRISTMAS

JINGLE BELLS

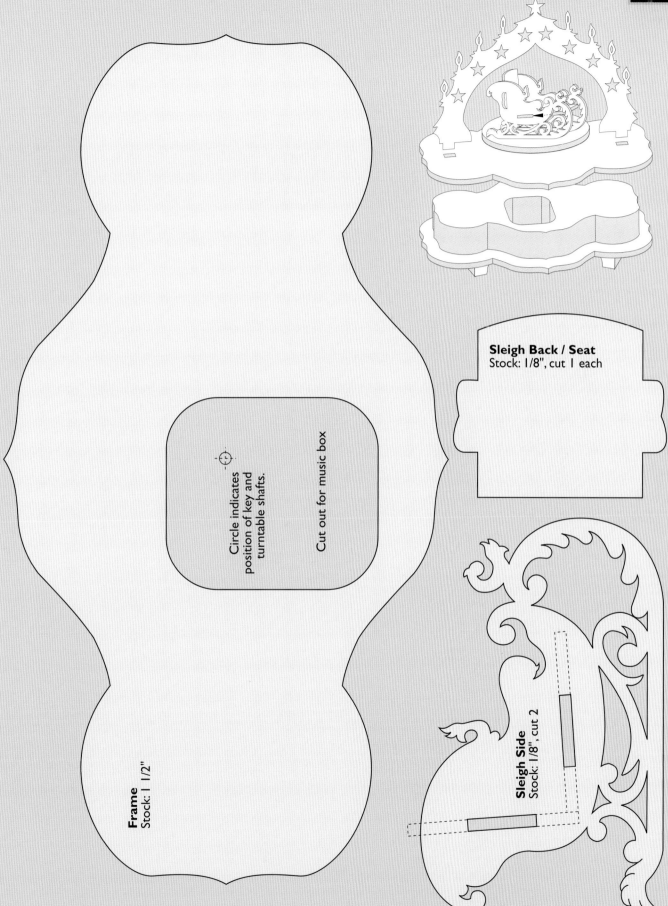

Circle indicates position of key and turntable shafts.

Cut out for music box

Frame
Stock: 1 1/2"

Sleigh Back / Seat
Stock: 1/8", cut 1 each

Sleigh Ride

Sleigh Side
Stock: 1/8", cut 2

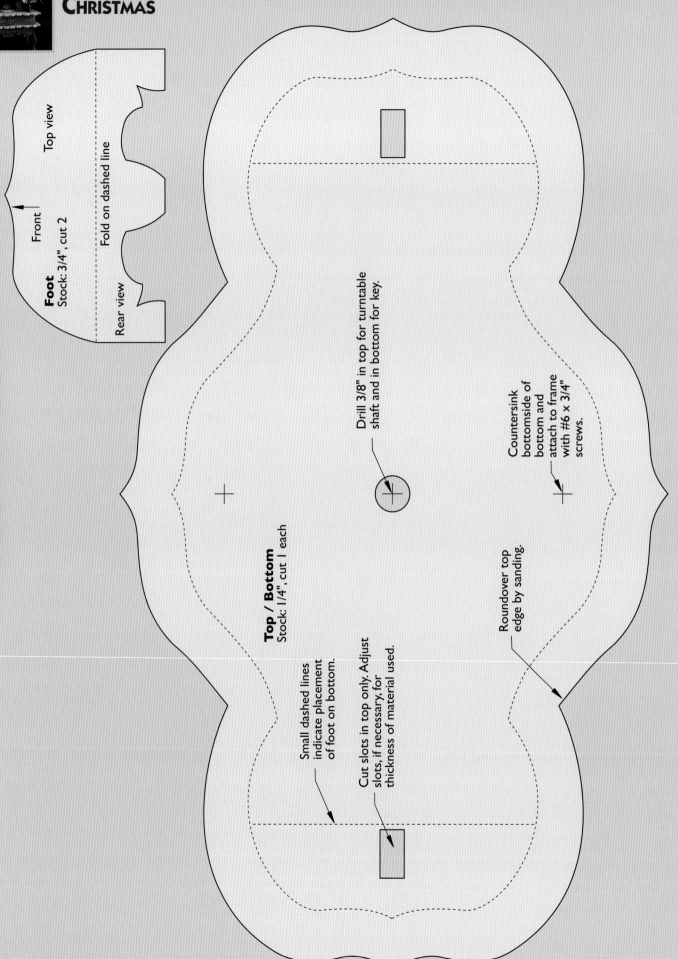

Sleigh Ride

Foot
Stock: 3/4", cut 2

Top view

Front

Fold on dashed line

Rear view

Drill 3/8" in top for turntable
shaft and in bottom for key.

Countersink
bottomside of
bottom and
attach to frame
with #6 x 3/4"
screws.

Top / Bottom
Stock: 1/4", cut 1 each

Roundover top
edge by sanding.

Small dashed lines
indicate placement
of foot on bottom.

Cut slots in top only. Adjust
slots, if necessary, for
thickness of material used.

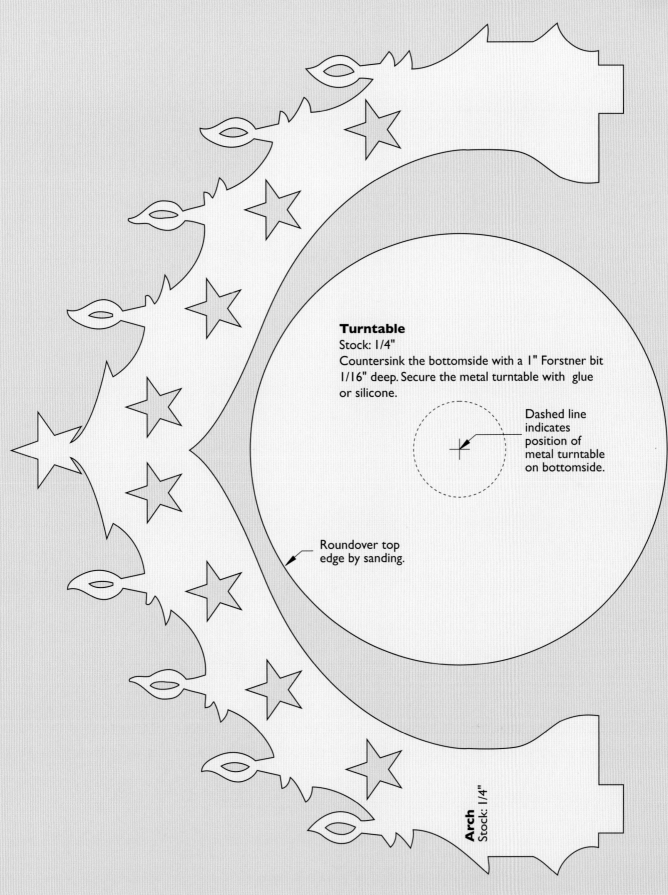

Turntable
Stock: 1/4"
Countersink the bottomside with a 1" Forstner bit
1/16" deep. Secure the metal turntable with glue
or silicone.

Dashed line
indicates
position of
metal turntable
on bottomside.

Roundover top
edge by sanding.

Arch
Stock: 1/4"

CHRISTMAS

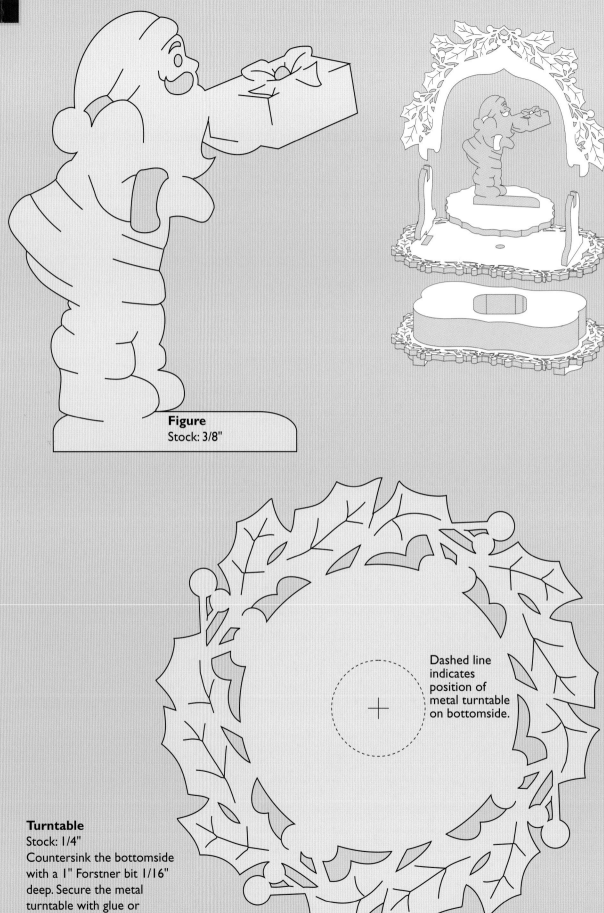

Figure
Stock: 3/8"

Dashed line
indicates
position of
metal turntable
on bottomside.

Turntable
Stock: 1/4"
Countersink the bottomside
with a 1" Forstner bit 1/16"
deep. Secure the metal
turntable with glue or
silicone.

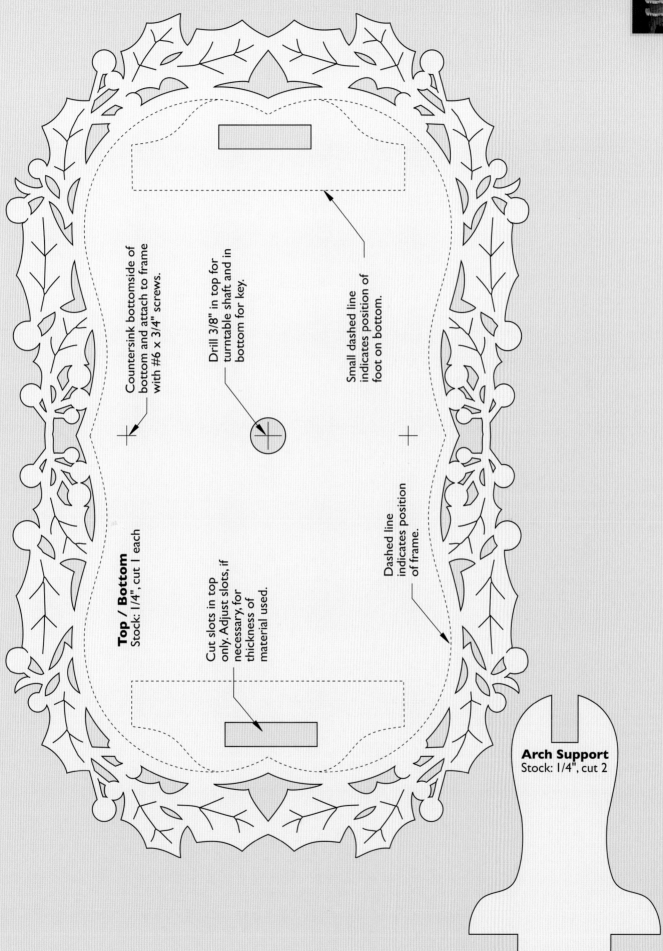

Countersink bottomside of bottom and attach to frame with #6 x 3/4" screws.

Drill 3/8" in top for turntable shaft and in bottom for key.

Small dashed line indicates position of foot on bottom.

Top / Bottom
Stock: 1/4", cut 1 each

Cut slots in top only. Adjust slots, if necessary, for thickness of material used.

Dashed line indicates position of frame.

Arch Support
Stock: 1/4", cut 2

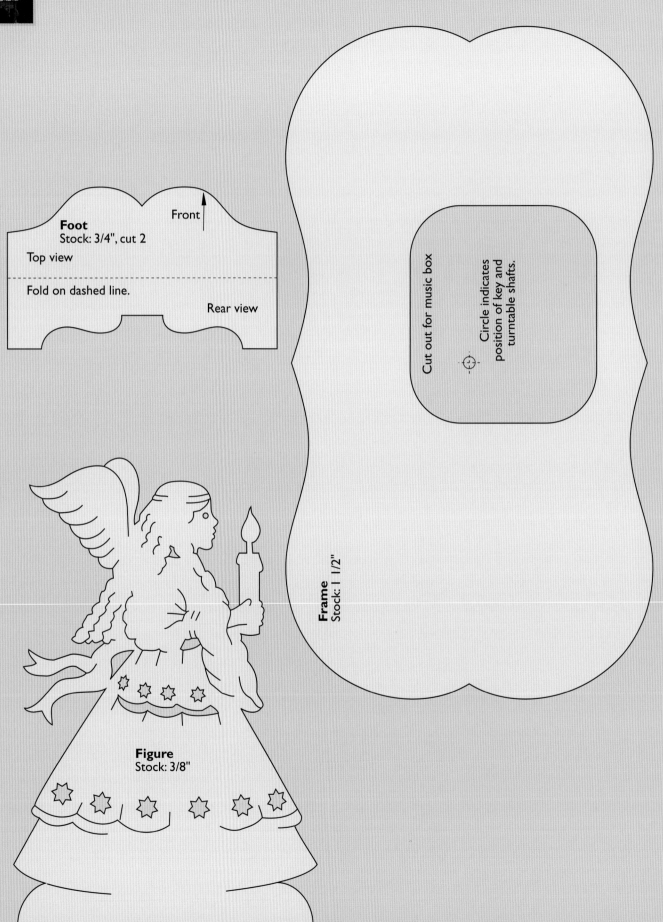

Foot
Stock: 3/4", cut 2

Top view

Front

Fold on dashed line.

Rear view

Cut out for music box

Circle indicates position of key and turntable shafts.

Frame
Stock: 1 1/2"

Figure
Stock: 3/8"

Arch
Stock: 1/4"

Figure
Stock: 3/8"

MOTHER'S DAY AND FATHER'S DAY

Figure
Stock: 3/8"

Frame
Stock: 1 1/2"

Cut out for music box

Circle indicates position of key and turntable shafts.

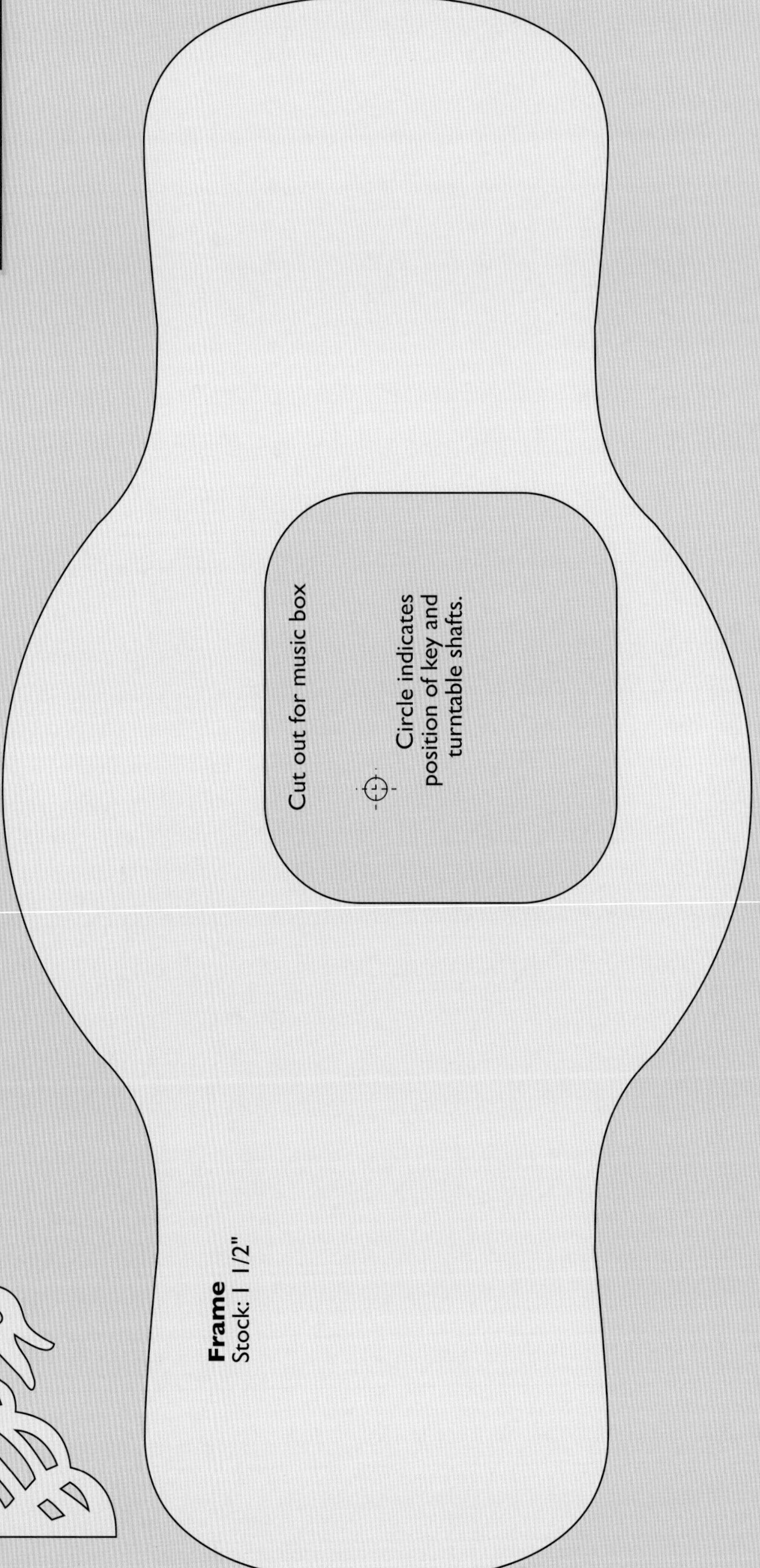

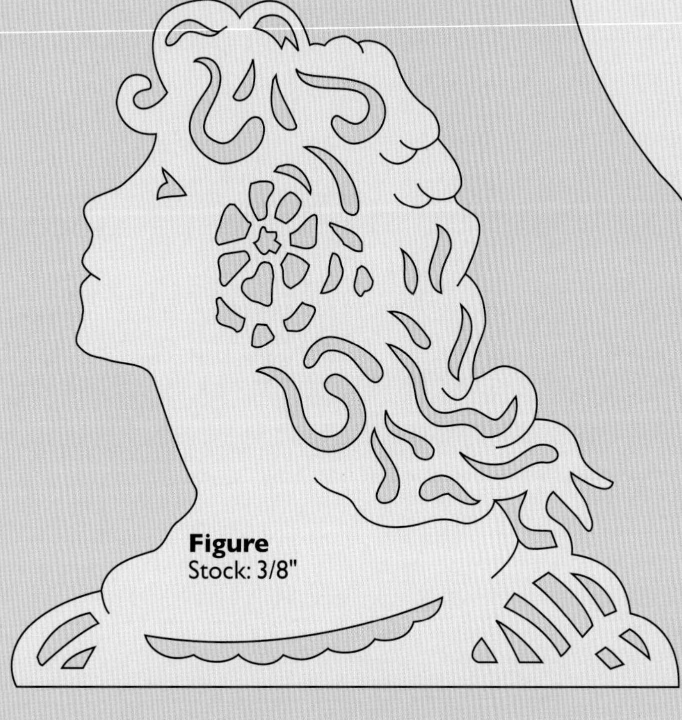

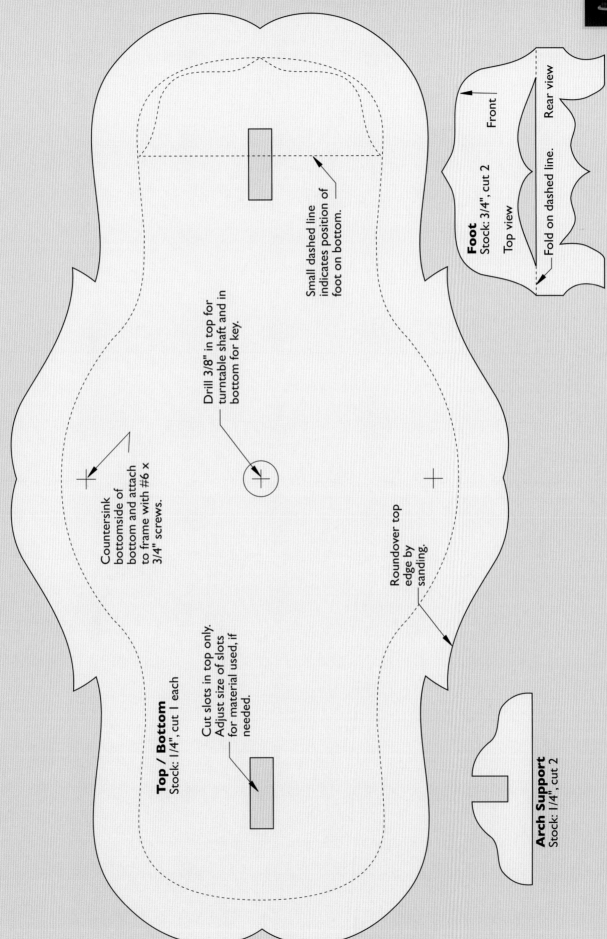

Foot
Stock: 3/4", cut 2

Front

Top view

Rear view

Fold on dashed line.

Small dashed line indicates position of foot on bottom.

Drill 3/8" in top for turntable shaft and in bottom for key.

Countersink bottomside of bottom and attach to frame with #6 x 3/4" screws.

Roundover top edge by sanding.

Top / Bottom
Stock: 1/4", cut 1 each

Cut slots in top only. Adjust size of slots for material used, if needed.

Arch Support
Stock: 1/4", cut 2

MOTHER'S DAY AND FATHER'S DAY

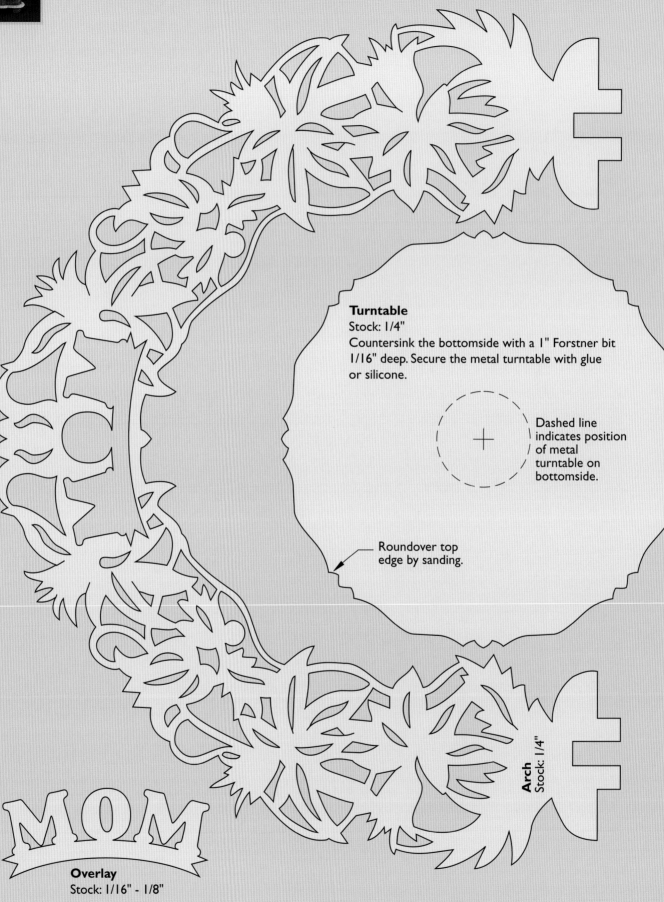

Turntable
Stock: 1/4"
Countersink the bottomside with a 1" Forstner bit 1/16" deep. Secure the metal turntable with glue or silicone.

Dashed line indicates position of metal turntable on bottomside.

Roundover top edge by sanding.

Arch
Stock: 1/4"

Overlay
Stock: 1/16" - 1/8"

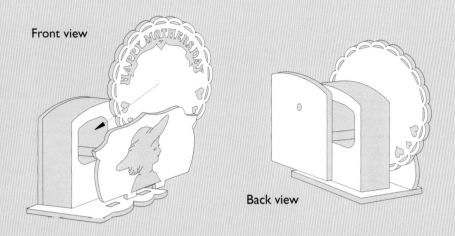

Front view

Back view

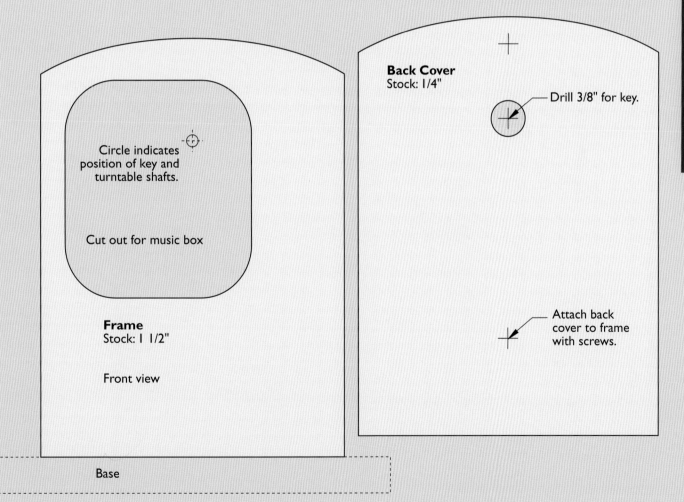

Circle indicates position of key and turntable shafts.

Cut out for music box

Frame
Stock: 1 1/2"

Front view

Base

Back Cover
Stock: 1/4"

Drill 3/8" for key.

Attach back cover to frame with screws.

Happy Mother's Day

MOTHER'S DAY AND FATHER'S DAY

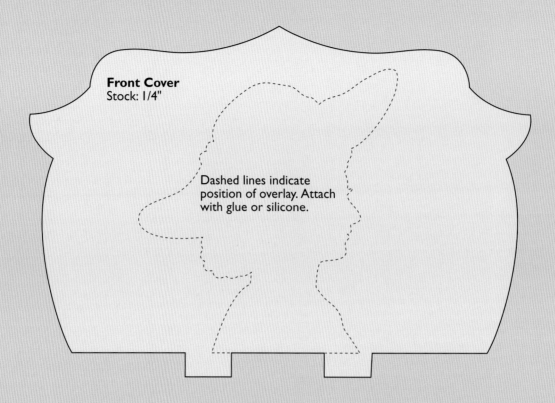

Front Cover
Stock: 1/4"

Dashed lines indicate position of overlay. Attach with glue or silicone.

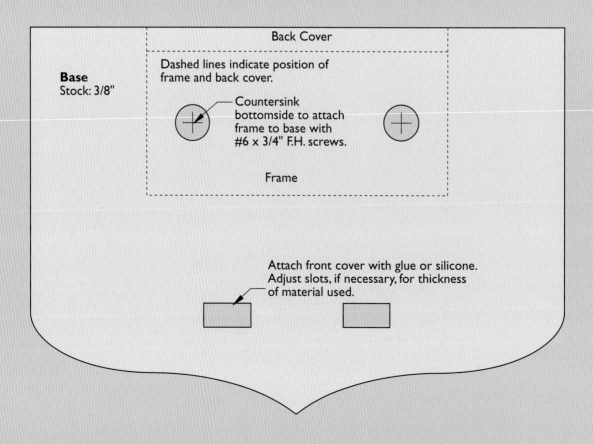

Back Cover

Dashed lines indicate position of frame and back cover.

Base
Stock: 3/8"

Countersink bottomside to attach frame to base with #6 x 3/4" F.H. screws.

Frame

Attach front cover with glue or silicone. Adjust slots, if necessary, for thickness of material used.

Happy Mother's Day

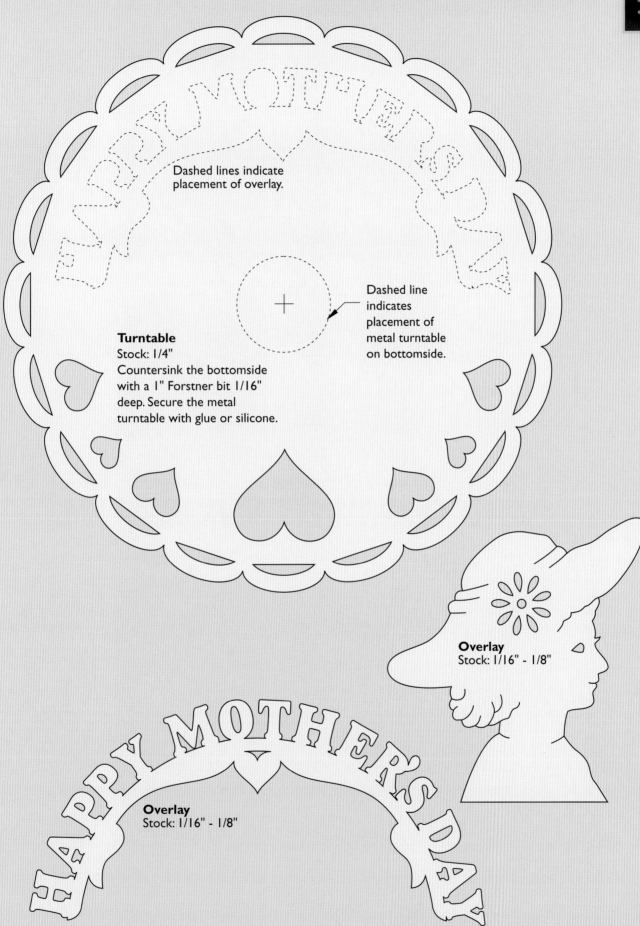

Dashed lines indicate placement of overlay.

Dashed line indicates placement of metal turntable on bottomside.

Turntable
Stock: 1/4"
Countersink the bottomside with a 1" Forstner bit 1/16" deep. Secure the metal turntable with glue or silicone.

Overlay
Stock: 1/16" - 1/8"

Overlay
Stock: 1/16" - 1/8"

Happy Mother's Day

Figure
Stock: 3/8"

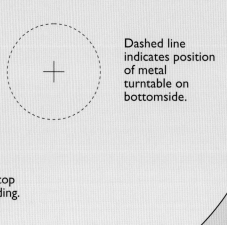

Turntable
Stock: 1/4"
Countersink the bottomside with a 1" Forstner
bit 1/16" deep. Secure the metal turntable with
glue or silicone.

Dashed line
indicates position
of metal
turntable on
bottomside.

Roundover top
edge by sanding.

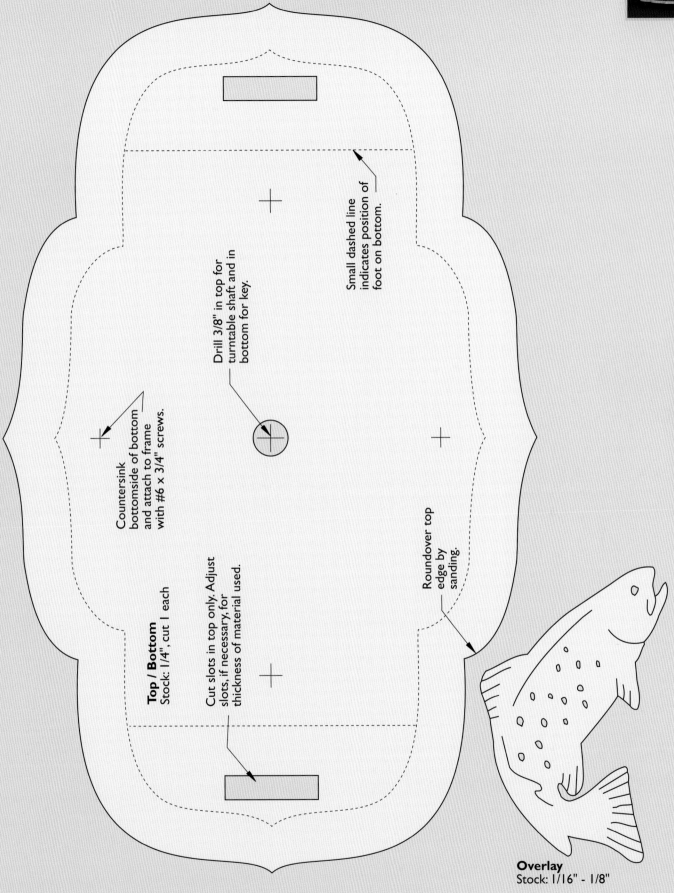

Small dashed line indicates position of foot on bottom.

Drill 3/8" in top for turntable shaft and in bottom for key.

Countersink bottomside of bottom and attach to frame with #6 x 3/4" screws.

Top / Bottom
Stock: 1/4", cut 1 each

Cut slots in top only. Adjust slots, if necessary, for thickness of material used.

Roundover top edge by sanding.

Overlay
Stock: 1/16" - 1/8"

For Dad

Overlay
Stock: 1/16" - 1/8"

Cut out for music box

Circle indicates position of key and turntable shafts.

Top view

Front

Rear view

Fold on dashed line.

Foot
Stock: 3/4", cut 2

Frame
Stock: 1 1/2"

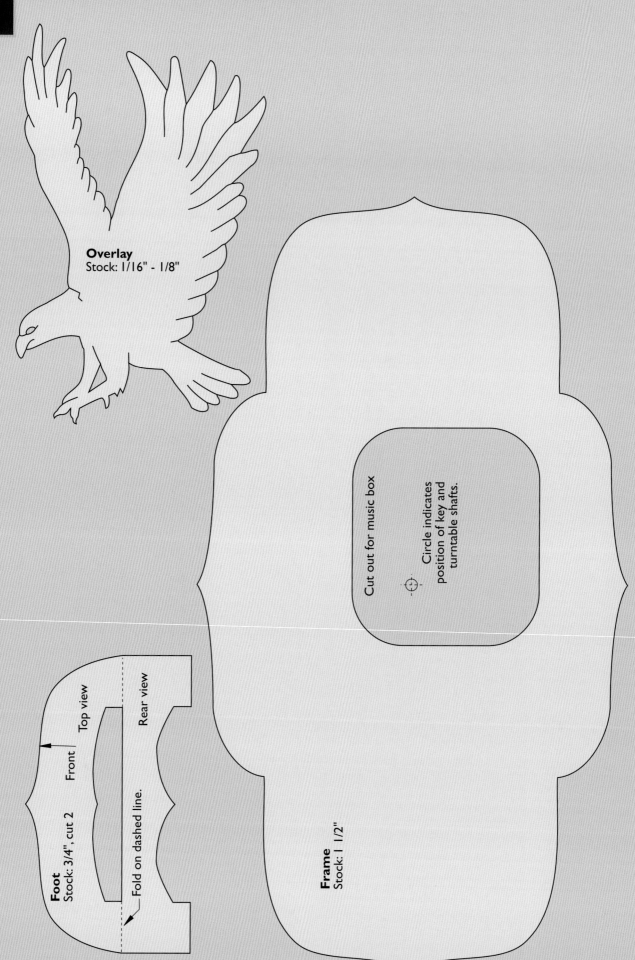

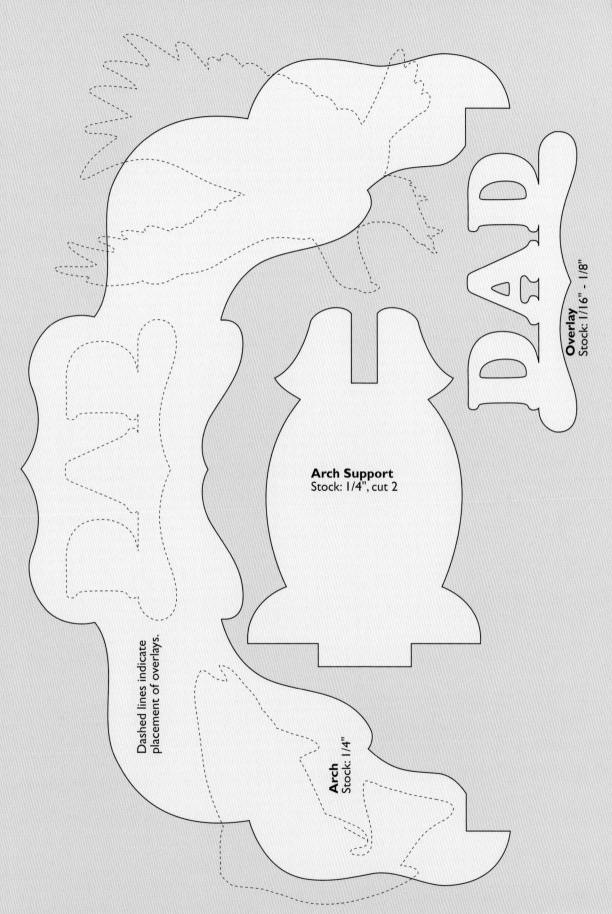

Overlay
Stock: 1/16" - 1/8"

Arch Support
Stock: 1/4", cut 2

Dashed lines indicate
placement of overlays.

Arch
Stock: 1/4"

MOTHER'S DAY AND FATHER'S DAY

Back Cover
Stock: 1/4"

Drill 3/8" for key.

Attach back
cover to frame
with screws.

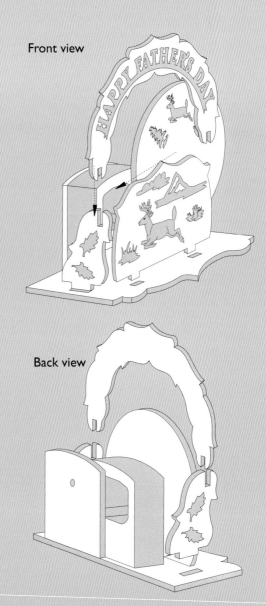

Front view

Back view

Cut out for music box

Circle indicates
position of key and
turntable shafts.

Frame
Stock: 1 1/2"

Front view

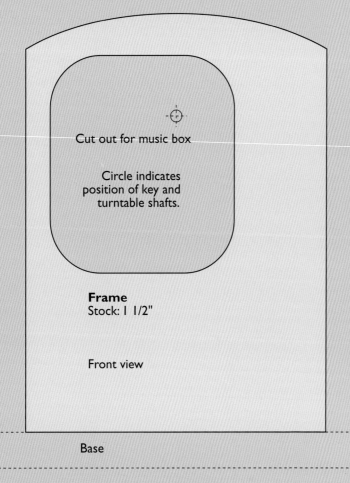

Base

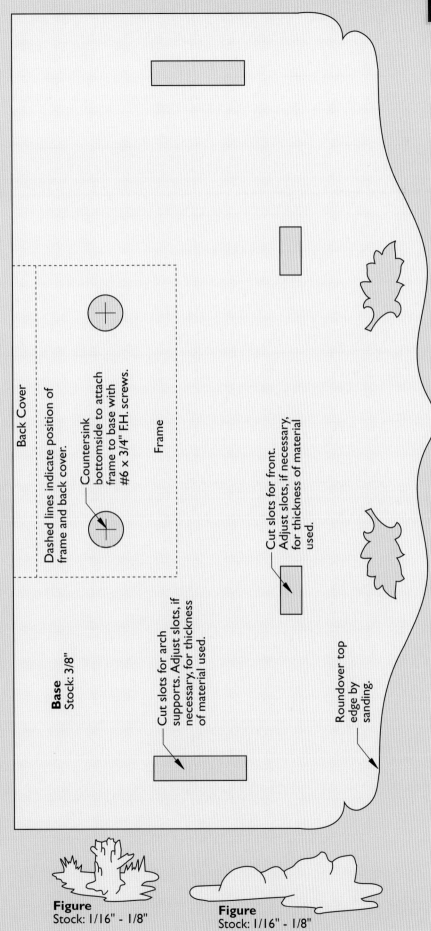

Back Cover

Dashed lines indicate position of frame and back cover.

Countersink bottomside to attach frame to base with #6 x 3/4" F.H. screws.

Frame

Base
Stock: 3/8"

Cut slots for front. Adjust slots, if necessary, for thickness of material used.

Cut slots for arch supports. Adjust slots, if necessary, for thickness of material used.

Roundover top edge by sanding.

Figure
Stock: 1/16" - 1/8"

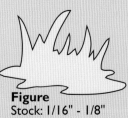

Figure
Stock: 1/16" - 1/8"

Figure
Stock: 1/16" - 1/8"

Figure
Stock: 1/16" - 1/8"

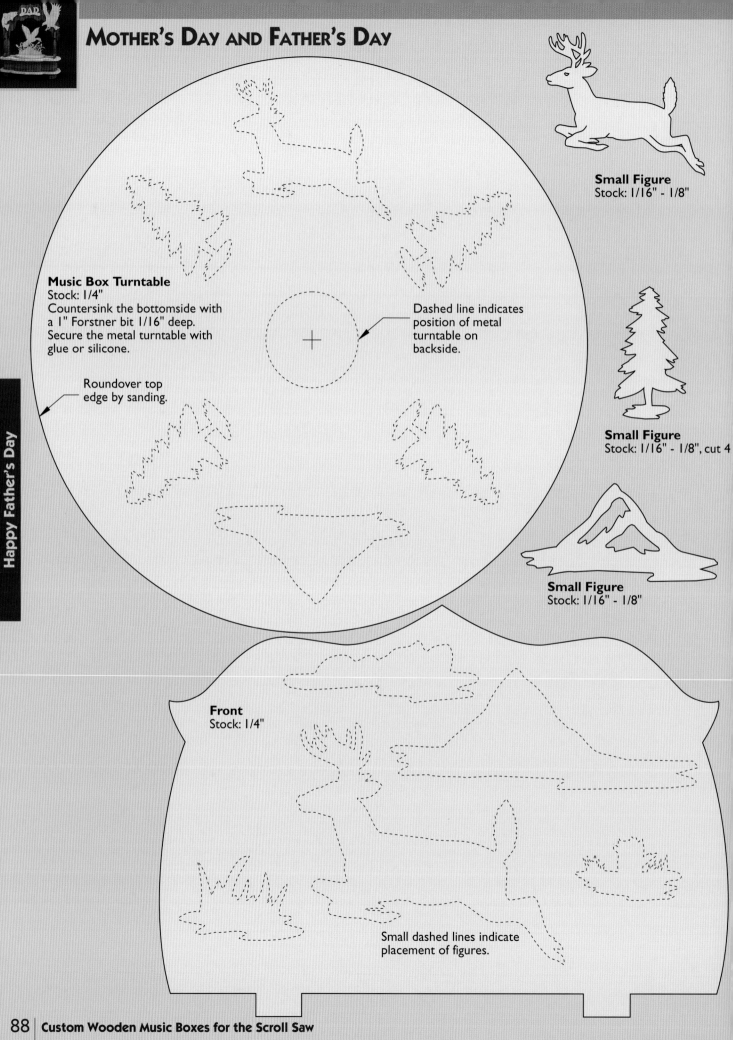

Small Figure
Stock: 1/16" - 1/8"

Music Box Turntable
Stock: 1/4"
Countersink the bottomside with a 1" Forstner bit 1/16" deep. Secure the metal turntable with glue or silicone.

Dashed line indicates position of metal turntable on backside.

Roundover top edge by sanding.

Small Figure
Stock: 1/16" - 1/8", cut 4

Small Figure
Stock: 1/16" - 1/8"

Front
Stock: 1/4"

Small dashed lines indicate placement of figures.

Dashed line indicates placement of top overlay.

Front

Figure
Stock: 1/16" - 1/8"

Arch Support
Stock: 1/4", cut 2

Top Overlay
Stock: 1/16" - 1/8"

Arch
Stock: 1/4"

HAPPY FATHER'S DAY

RELIGIOUS

Dashed lines indicate placement of clouds on figure.

Cloud
Stock: 1/8" - 3/8", cut 2

Turntable
Stock: 1/4"
Countersink the bottomside with a 1" Forstner bit 1/16" deep. Secure the metal turntable with glue or silicone.

Dashed line indicates position of metal turntable on backside.

Roundover top edge by sanding.

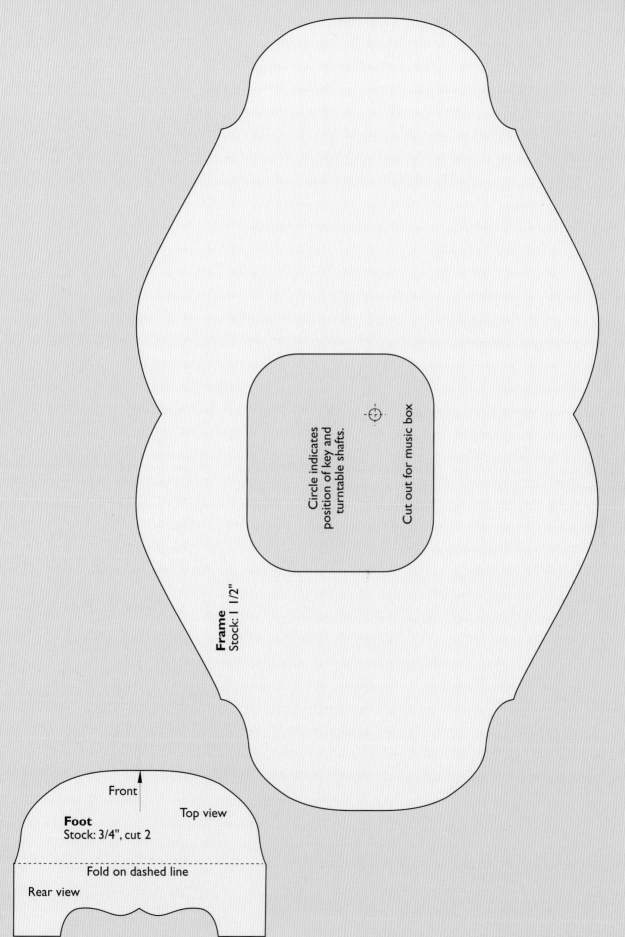

Frame
Stock: 1 1/2"

Circle indicates
position of key and
turntable shafts.

Cut out for music box

Top view

Front

Foot
Stock: 3/4", cut 2

Fold on dashed line

Rear view

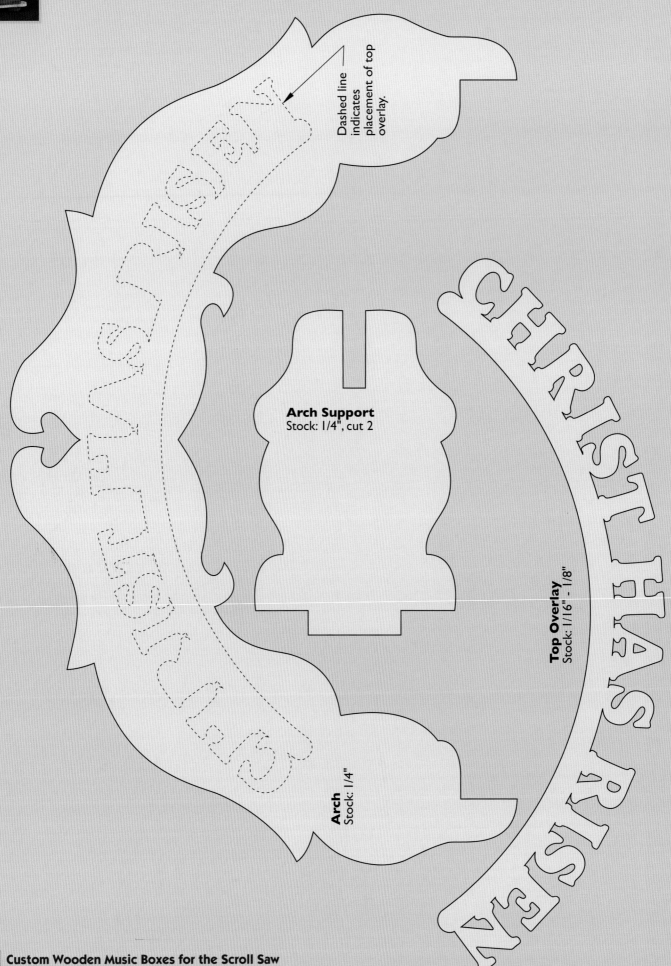

Dashed line indicates placement of top overlay.

Arch Support
Stock: 1/4", cut 2

Arch
Stock: 1/4"

Top Overlay
Stock: 1/16" – 1/8"

Christ Has Risen

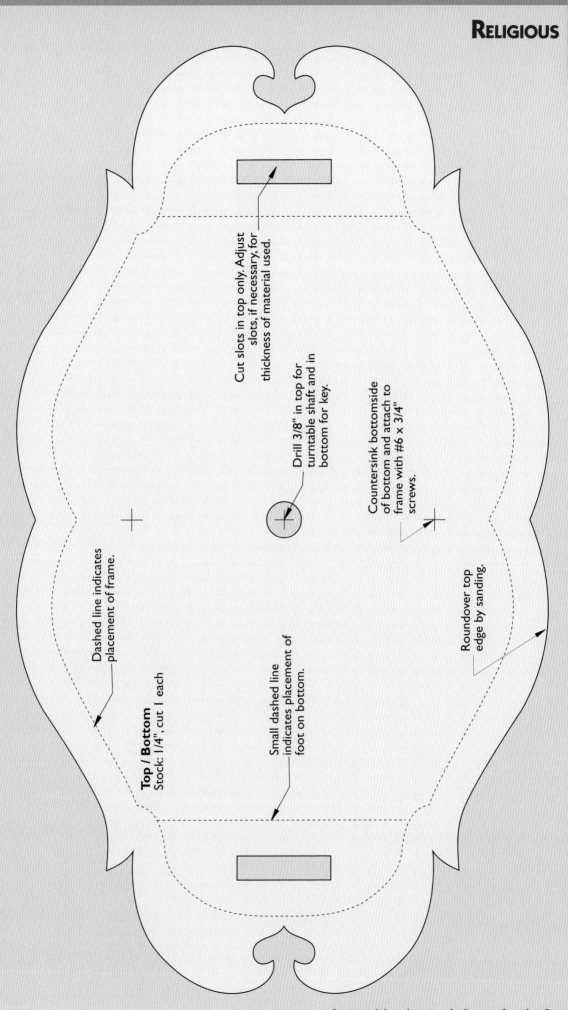

Cut slots in top only. Adjust slots, if necessary, for thickness of material used.

Drill 3/8" in top for turntable shaft and in bottom for key.

Countersink bottomside of bottom and attach to frame with #6 x 3/4" screws.

Dashed line indicates placement of frame.

Top / Bottom
Stock: 1/4", cut 1 each

Small dashed line indicates placement of foot on bottom.

Roundover top edge by sanding.

Christ Has Risen

RELIGIOUS

Joyful

Arch Support
Stock: 1/4", cut 2

+ Top +

Attach arch support to
top with glue and
finishing nails.

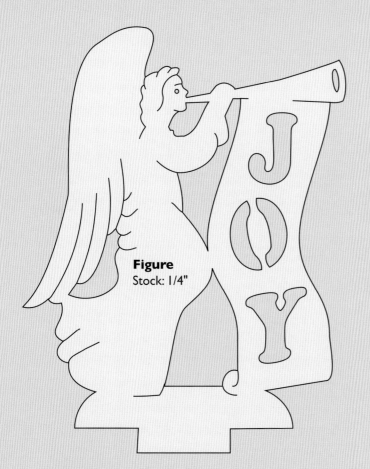

Figure
Stock: 1/4"

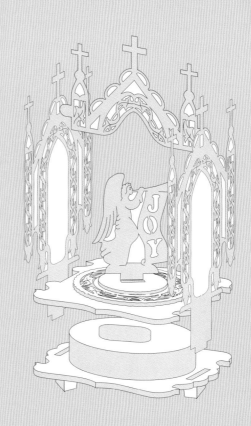

Turntable
Stock: 1/4"
Countersink the bottomside with a 1" Forstner bit 1/16" deep. Secure the metal turntable with glue or silicone.

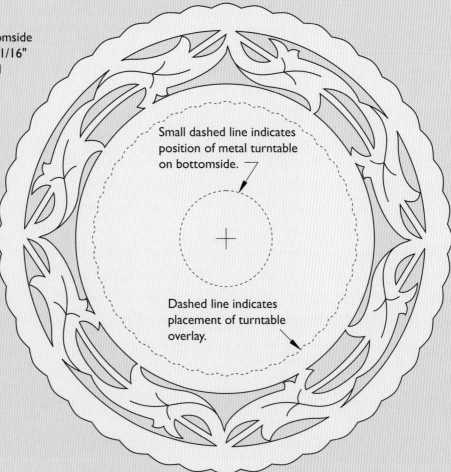

Small dashed line indicates position of metal turntable on bottomside.

Dashed line indicates placement of turntable overlay.

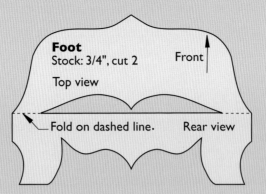

Foot
Stock: 3/4", cut 2

Top view

Front

Fold on dashed line.   Rear view

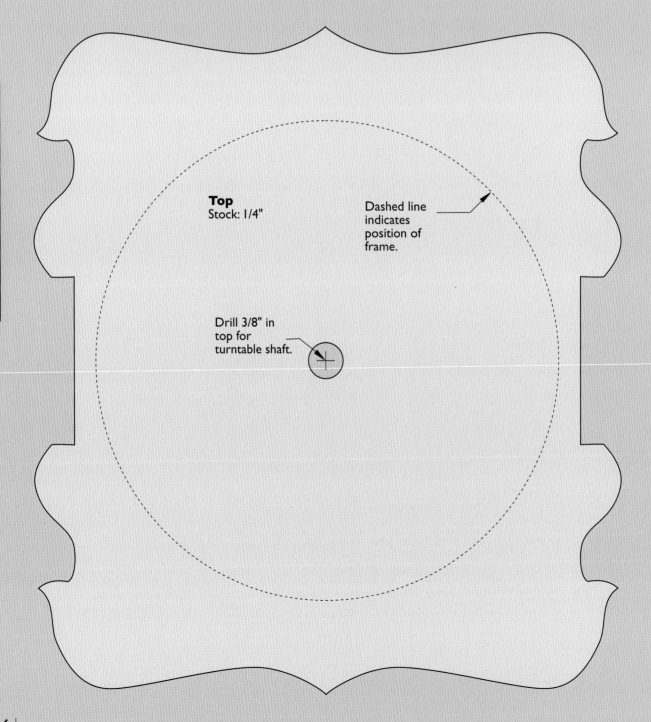

Top
Stock: 1/4"

Dashed line
indicates
position of
frame.

Drill 3/8" in
top for
turntable shaft.

Joyful

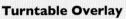

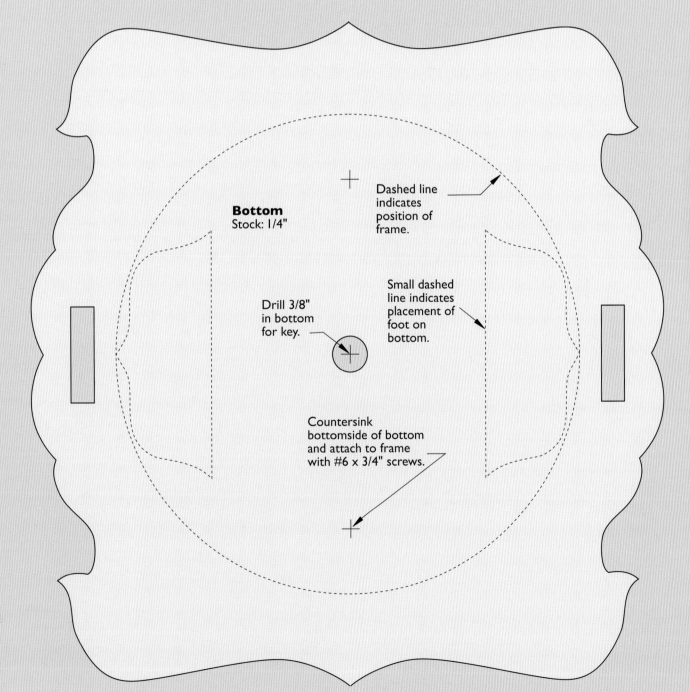

Turntable Overlay
Stock: 1/4"

Adjust slot, if
necessary, for
thickness of
material used.

Bottom
Stock: 1/4"

Dashed line
indicates
position of
frame.

Small dashed
line indicates
placement of
foot on
bottom.

Drill 3/8"
in bottom
for key.

Countersink
bottomside of bottom
and attach to frame
with #6 x 3/4" screws.

Joyful

Arch
Stock: 1/4"

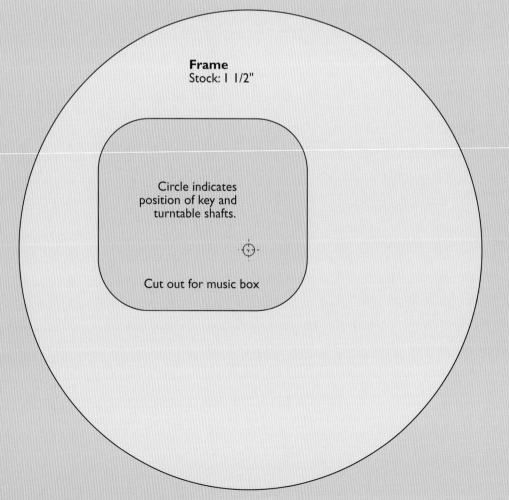

Frame
Stock: 1 1/2"

Circle indicates
position of key and
turntable shafts.

Cut out for music box

Cathedral Music Box		
Description	**Item**	**Qty**
Front Wall	A	1
Back Wall	B	1
Wall Anchor	C	4
Side Wall	D	2
Front & Back Base	E	1 each
Base Side	F	2
Front & Back Spire	G	1 each
Spire Side	H	2
Floor	I	1
Bottom Support	J	2
Side Support	K	2
Ceiling	L	1
Turntable	M	1
Turntable Overlay	N	1
Figure	O	1

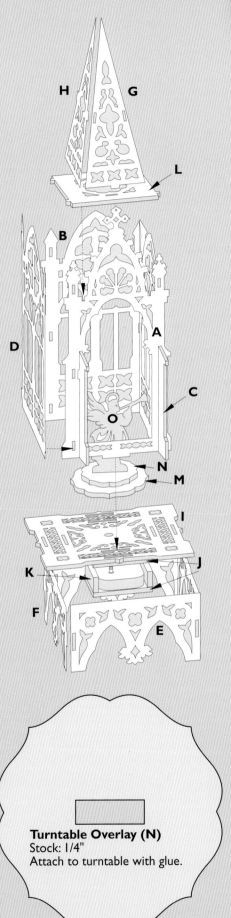

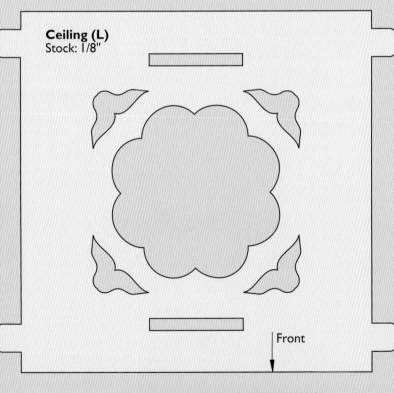

Ceiling (L)
Stock: 1/8"

Front

Bottom Support

Side Support (K)
Stock: 1/4", cut 2

Bottom Support

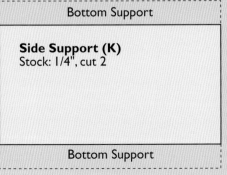

Turntable Overlay (N)
Stock: 1/4"
Attach to turntable with glue.

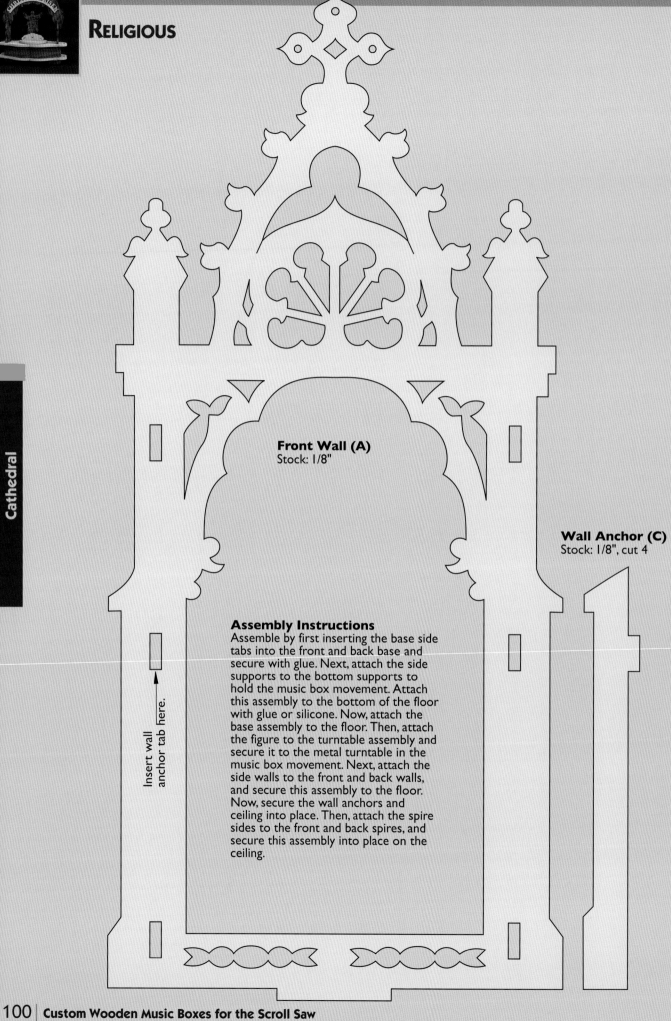

Front Wall (A)
Stock: 1/8"

Wall Anchor (C)
Stock: 1/8", cut 4

Insert wall anchor tab here.

Assembly Instructions
Assemble by first inserting the base side tabs into the front and back base and secure with glue. Next, attach the side supports to the bottom supports to hold the music box movement. Attach this assembly to the bottom of the floor with glue or silicone. Now, attach the base assembly to the floor. Then, attach the figure to the turntable assembly and secure it to the metal turntable in the music box movement. Next, attach the side walls to the front and back walls, and secure this assembly to the floor. Now, secure the wall anchors and ceiling into place. Then, attach the spire sides to the front and back spires, and secure this assembly into place on the ceiling.

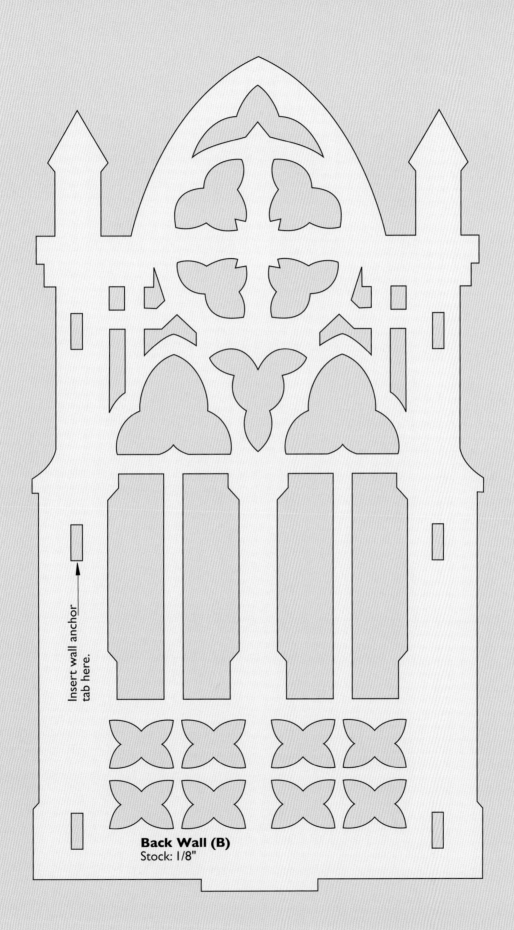

Insert wall anchor
tab here.

Back Wall (B)
Stock: 1/8"

Cathedral

Cathedral

Ceiling tab
fits here

Side Wall (D)
Stock: 1/8", cut 2

Base Side (F)
Stock: 1/8", cut 2

Figure (O)
Stock: 1/4"

Front & Back Base (E)
Stock: 1/8", cut 1 each

Front & Back Spire (G)
Stock: 1/8", cut 1 each

Spire Side (H)
Stock: 1/8", cut 2

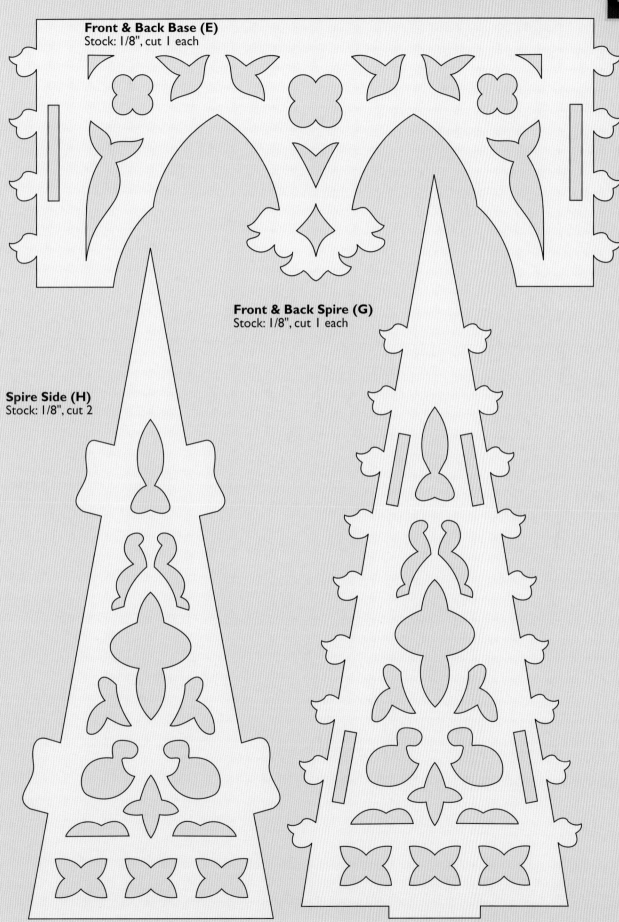

RELIGIOUS

Floor (I)
Stock: 1/4"

Insert back
wall tab here.

Dashed lines indicate
placement of bottom
support assembly. Attach
to bottomside of floor
with glue or silicone.

Insert base
side tabs here.

Drill 3/8"
turntable shaft.

Insert front
wall tab here.

Front

Turntable (M)
Stock: 1/4"
Countersink the bottomside with a 1" Forstner bit 1/16" deep.
Secure the metal turntable with glue or silicone.

Small dashed line
indicates position of
turntable overlay.

Dashed line
indicates position
of metal turntable
on bottomside.

Bottom Support (J)
Stock: 1/4", cut 2

Side Support

Side Support

Drill 3/8" for key.

Attach side
supports with glue
and finishing nails.

Cathedral

ROMANCE

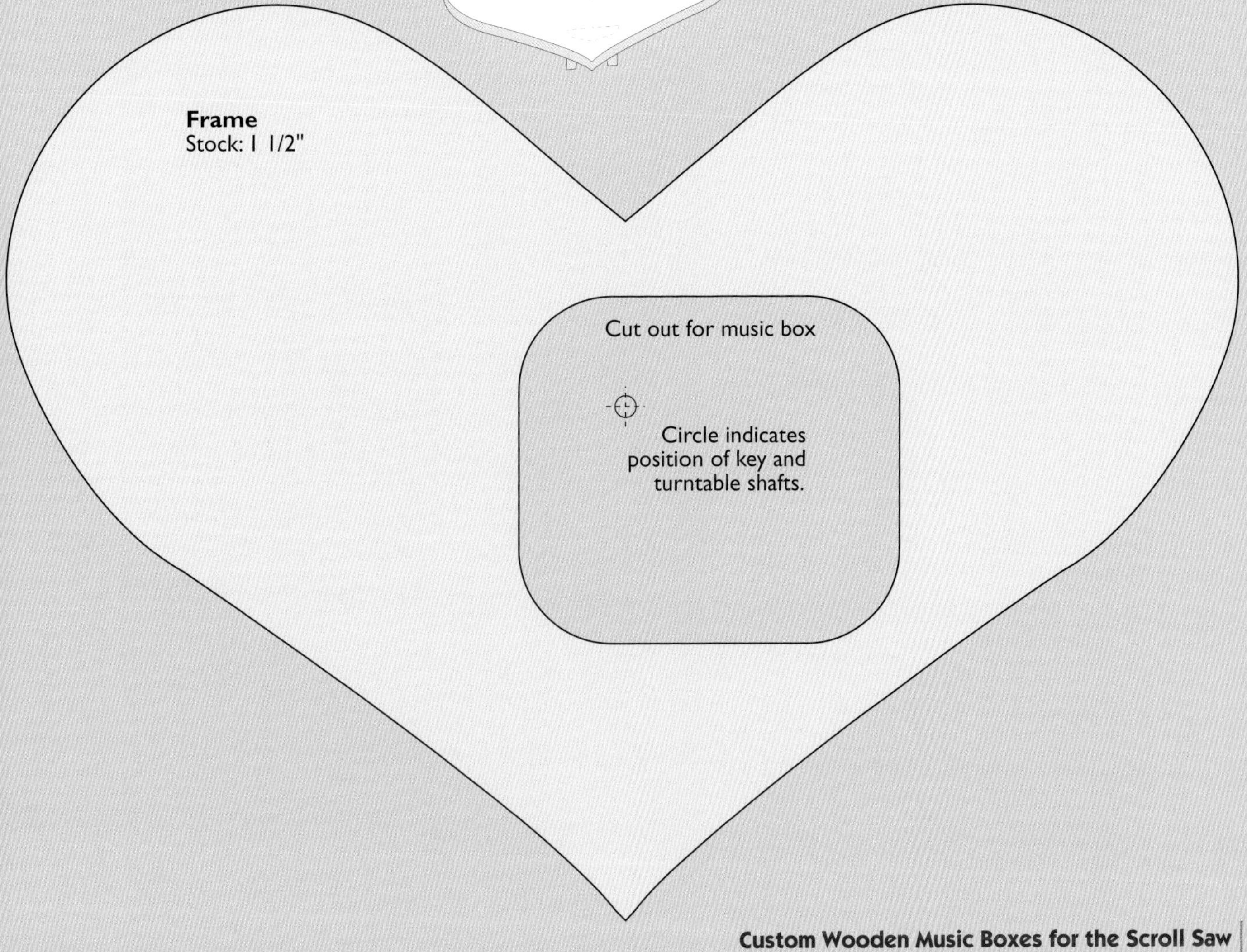

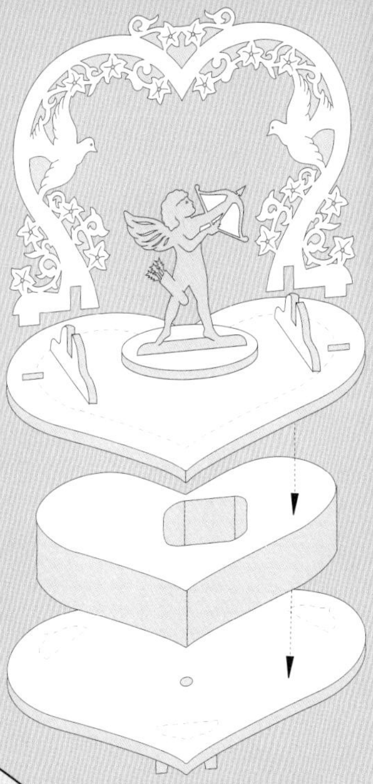

Frame
Stock: 1 1/2"

Cut out for music box

Circle indicates
position of key and
turntable shafts.

ROMANCE

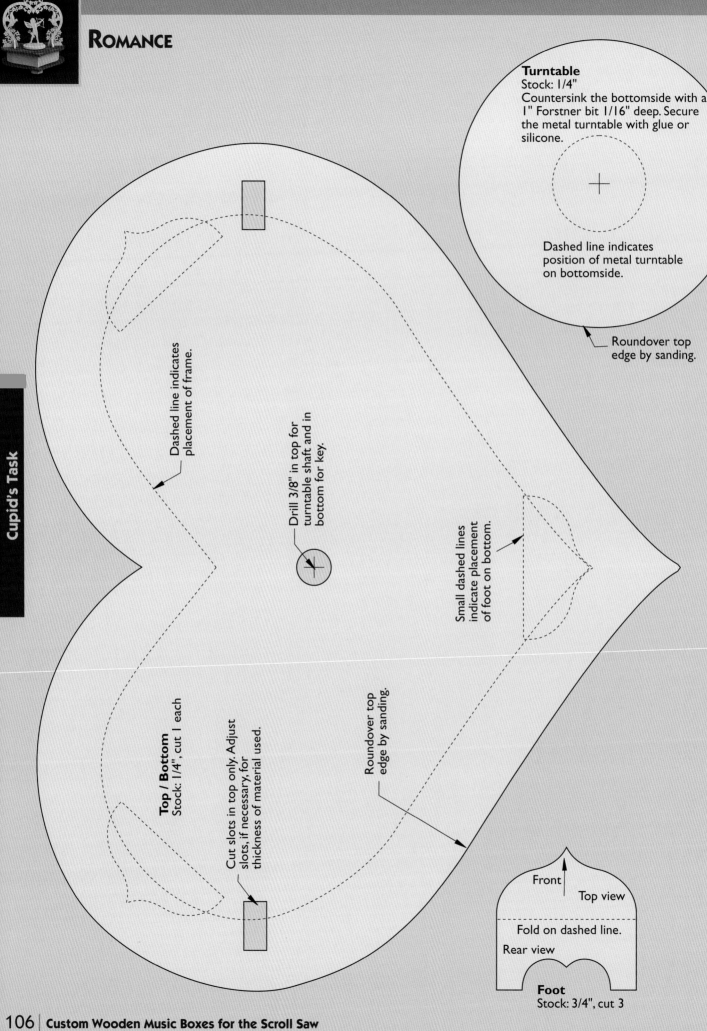

Turntable
Stock: 1/4"
Countersink the bottomside with a 1" Forstner bit 1/16" deep. Secure the metal turntable with glue or silicone.

Dashed line indicates position of metal turntable on bottomside.

Roundover top edge by sanding.

Dashed line indicates placement of frame.

Drill 3/8" in top for turntable shaft and in bottom for key.

Small dashed lines indicate placement of foot on bottom.

Top / Bottom
Stock: 1/4", cut 1 each

Cut slots in top only. Adjust slots, if necessary, for thickness of material used.

Roundover top edge by sanding.

Front

Top view

Fold on dashed line.

Rear view

Foot
Stock: 3/4", cut 3

Figure
Stock: 3/8"

Arch
Stock: 1/4"

Arch Support
Stock: 1/4", cut 2

Cupid's Task

ROMANCE

Foot
Stock: 3/4", cut 2

Front

Top view

Fold on dashed line.

Rear view

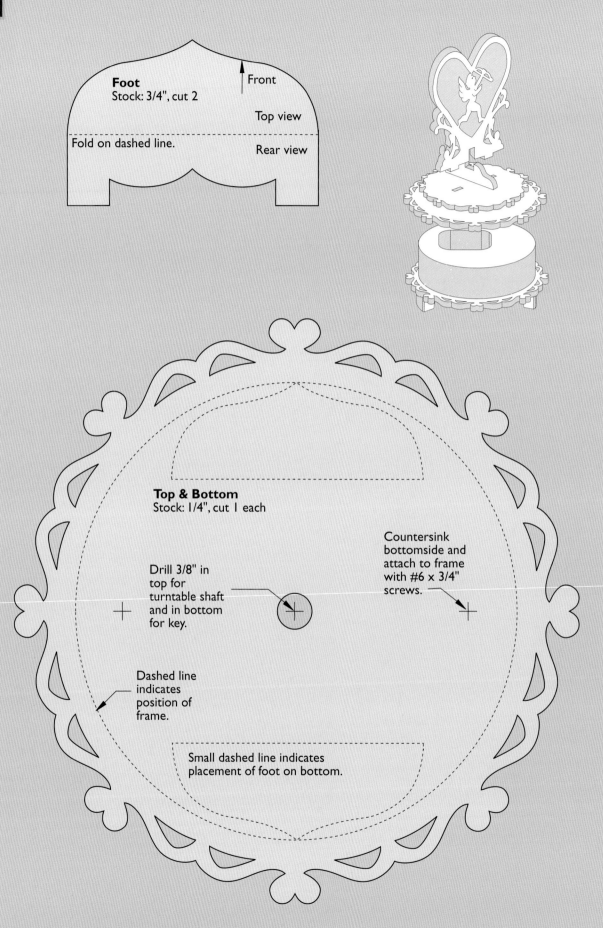

Top & Bottom
Stock: 1/4", cut 1 each

Countersink
bottomside and
attach to frame
with #6 x 3/4"
screws.

Drill 3/8" in
top for
turntable shaft
and in bottom
for key.

Dashed line
indicates
position of
frame.

Small dashed line indicates
placement of foot on bottom.

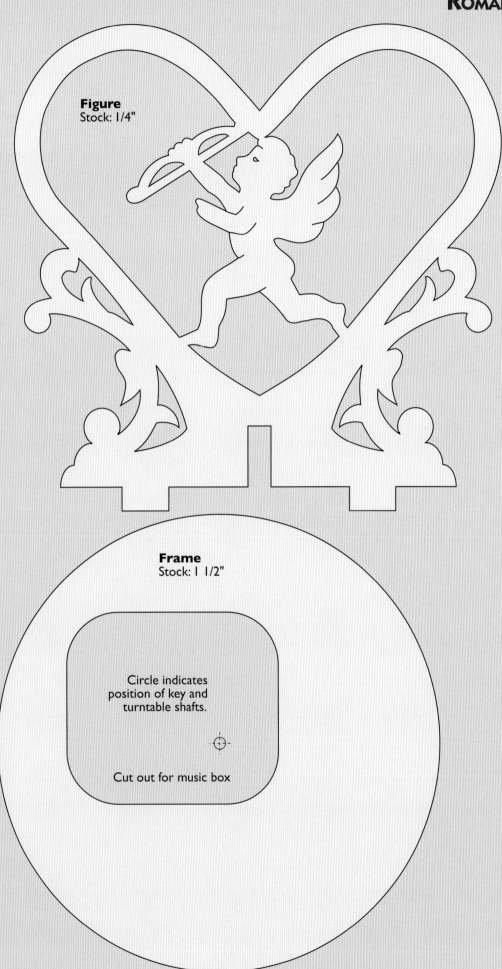

Figure
Stock: 1/4"

Frame
Stock: 1 1/2"

Circle indicates
position of key and
turntable shafts.

Cut out for music box

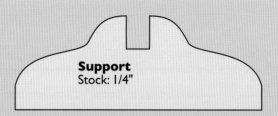

Support
Stock: 1/4"

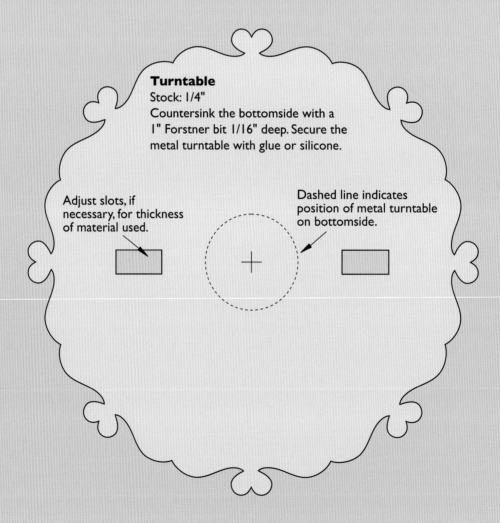

Turntable
Stock: 1/4"
Countersink the bottomside with a
1" Forstner bit 1/16" deep. Secure the
metal turntable with glue or silicone.

Adjust slots, if
necessary, for thickness
of material used.

Dashed line indicates
position of metal turntable
on bottomside.

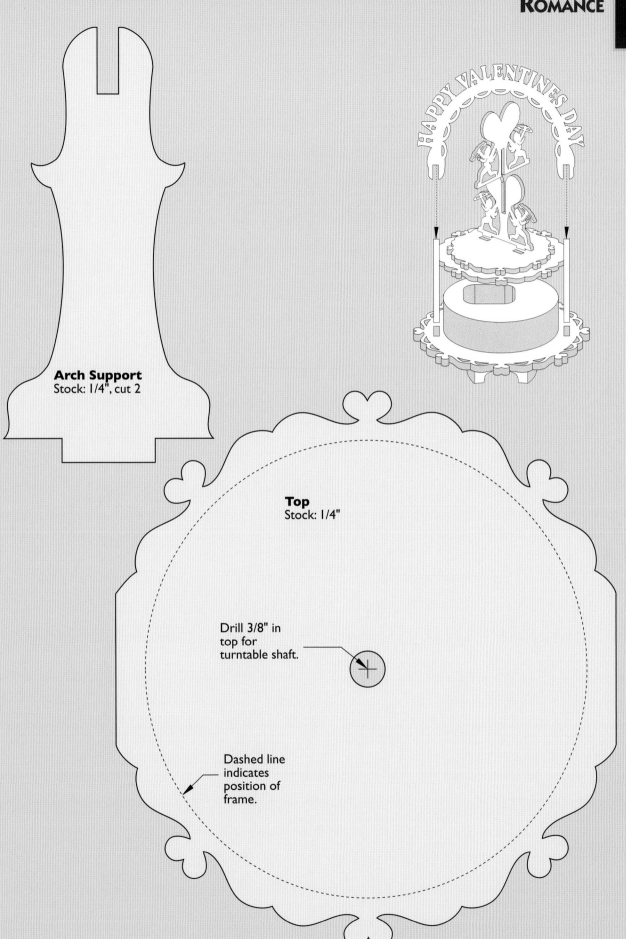

Arch Support
Stock: 1/4", cut 2

Top
Stock: 1/4"

Drill 3/8" in
top for
turntable shaft.

Dashed line
indicates
position of
frame.

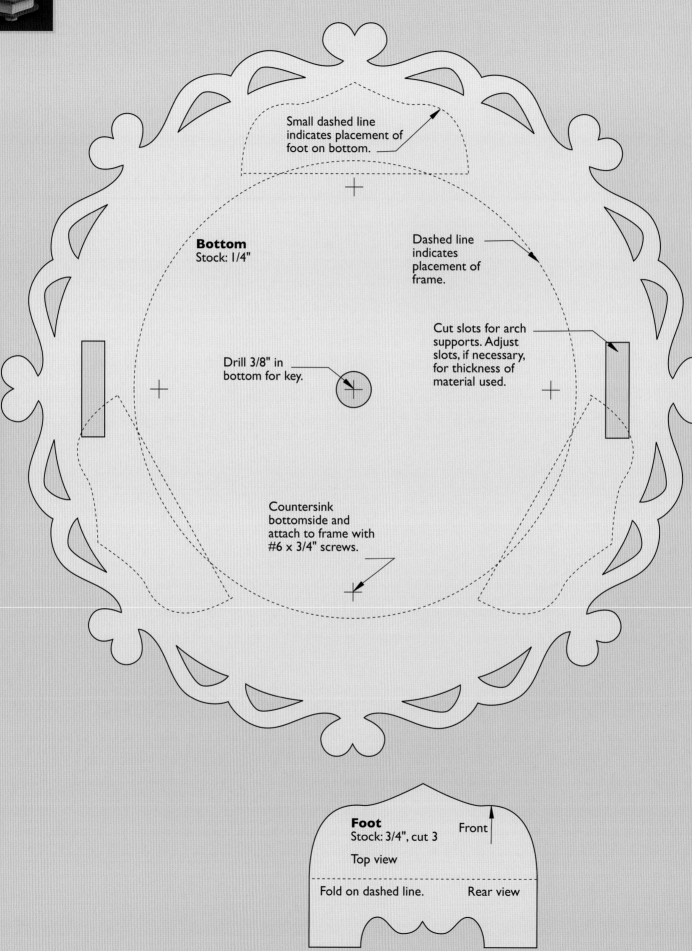

Small dashed line indicates placement of foot on bottom.

Bottom
Stock: 1/4"

Dashed line indicates placement of frame.

Drill 3/8" in bottom for key.

Cut slots for arch supports. Adjust slots, if necessary, for thickness of material used.

Countersink bottomside and attach to frame with #6 x 3/4" screws.

Foot
Stock: 3/4", cut 3

Top view

Front

Fold on dashed line.

Rear view

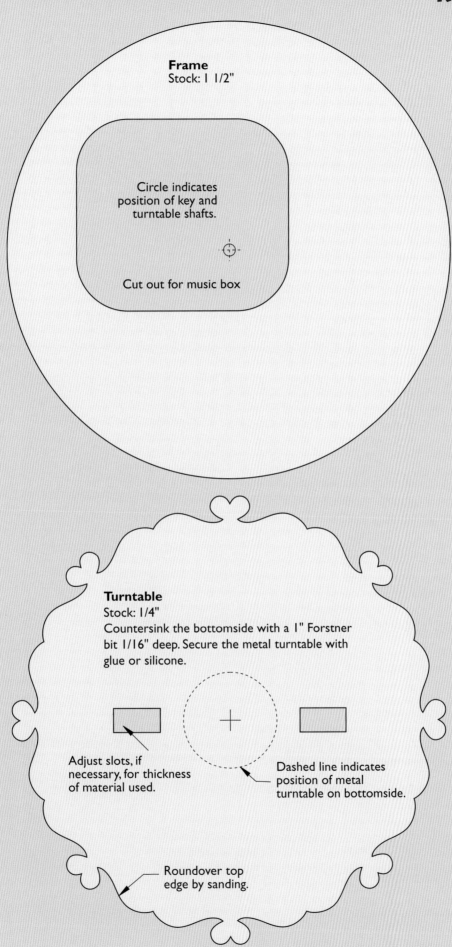

Frame
Stock: 1 1/2"

Circle indicates
position of key and
turntable shafts.

Cut out for music box

Turntable
Stock: 1/4"
Countersink the bottomside with a 1" Forstner
bit 1/16" deep. Secure the metal turntable with
glue or silicone.

Adjust slots, if
necessary, for thickness
of material used.

Dashed line indicates
position of metal
turntable on bottomside.

Roundover top
edge by sanding.

Arch
Stock: 1/4"

Figures
Stock: 1/4"

Figures
Stock: 1/4"

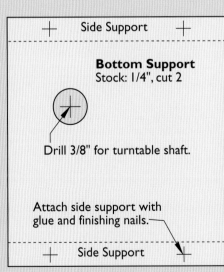

Base Support
Stock: 1/4"

Bottom Support

Side Support
Stock: 1/4", cut 2

Bottom Support

+ Side Support +

Bottom Support
Stock: 1/4", cut 2

Drill 3/8" for turntable shaft.

Attach side support with
glue and finishing nails.

+ Side Support +

Arch Support
Stock: 1/4", cut 2

Arch
Stock: 1/4"

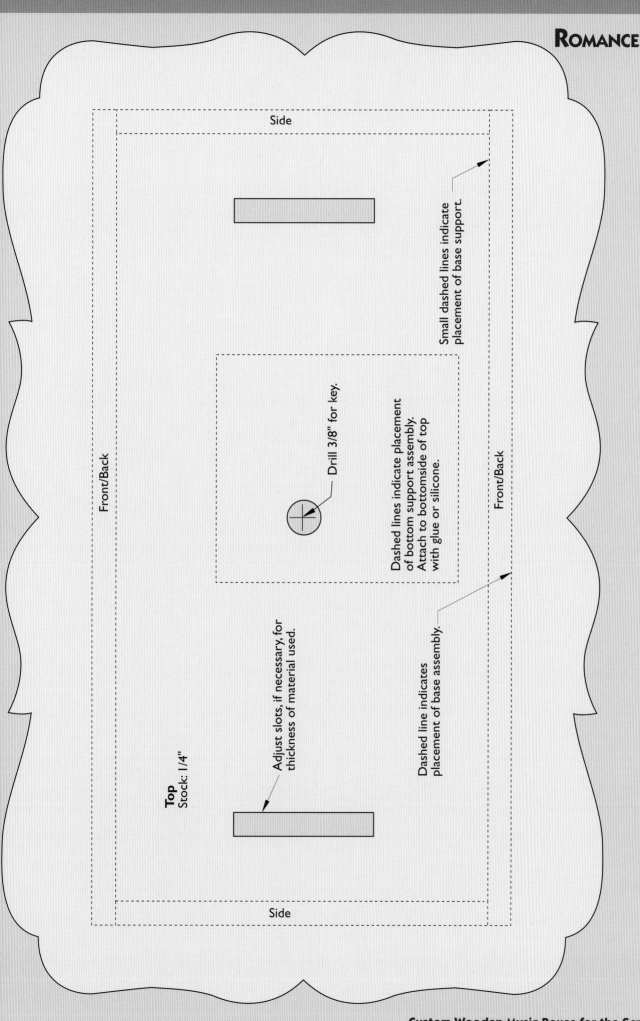

Side

Front/Back

Small dashed lines indicate placement of base support.

Drill 3/8" for key.

Dashed lines indicate placement of bottom support assembly. Attach to bottomside of top with glue or silicone.

Front/Back

Adjust slots, if necessary, for thickness of material used.

Top
Stock: 1/4"

Dashed line indicates placement of base assembly.

Side

Quiet Moments

Turntable
Stock: 1/4"
Countersink the bottomside with a
1" Forstner bit 1/16" deep. Secure the
metal turntable with glue or silicone.

Dashed line indicates
placement of
turntable overlay.

Turntable Overlay
Stock: 1/4"
Secure to the turntable with glue or silicone.

Adjust slot, if
necessary, for
thickness of
material used.

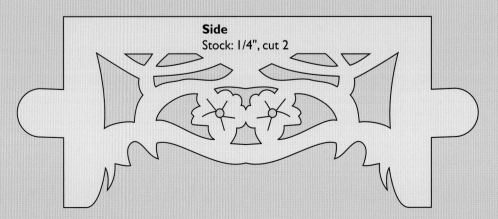

Side
Stock: 1/4", cut 2

Attach to base support with glue
and #18 x 5/8" finishing nails.

Front & Back
Stock: 1/4", cut 1 each

Figures
Stock: 1/4"

Quiet Moments

Turntable
Stock: 1/4"
Countersink the bottomside with a
1" Forstner bit 1/16" deep. Secure the metal
turntable with glue or silicone.

Adjust slots, if
necessary, for
thickness of
material used.

Dashed line
indicates position
of metal
turntable on
bottomside.

Foot
Stock: 3/4", cut 2
Top view

Fold on dashed line.
Rear view

Figure
Stock: 1/4"

Text Overlay
Stock: 1/16" - 1/8"

01

Arch
Stock: 1/4"

Fence
Stock: 1/4",
cut 2

23

Number Overlays
Stock: 1/16" - 1/8"

456789

Arch Support
Stock: 1/4", cut 2

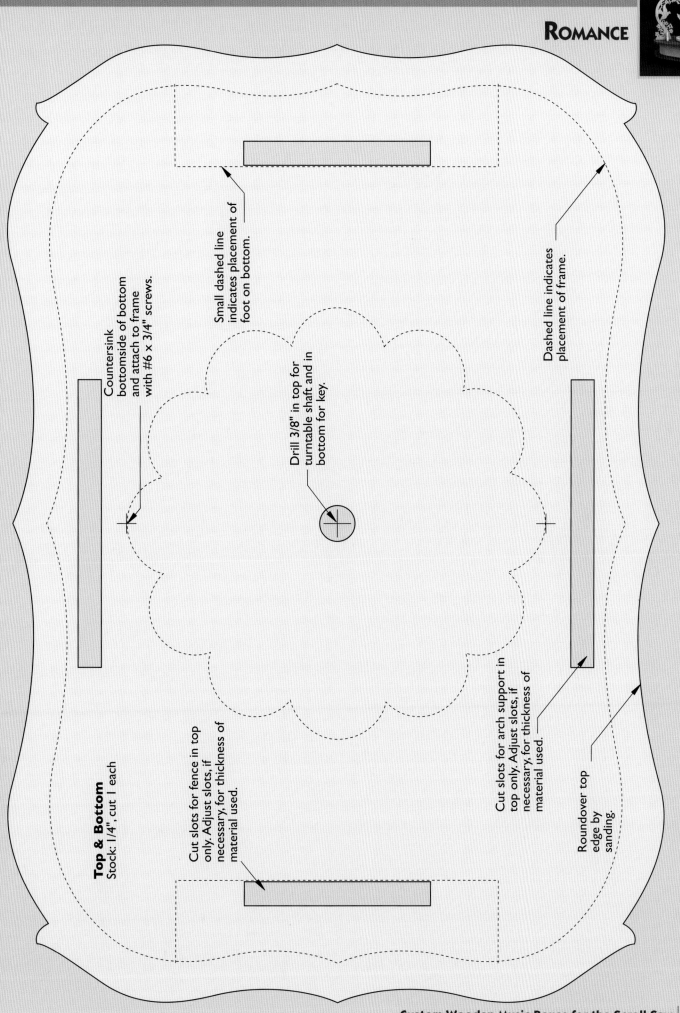

Countersink bottomside of bottom and attach to frame with #6 x 3/4" screws.

Small dashed line indicates placement of foot on bottom.

Dashed line indicates placement of frame.

Drill 3/8" in top for turntable shaft and in bottom for key.

Top & Bottom
Stock: 1/4", cut 1 each

Cut slots for fence in top only. Adjust slots, if necessary, for thickness of material used.

Cut slots for arch support in top only. Adjust slots, if necessary, for thickness of material used.

Roundover top edge by sanding.

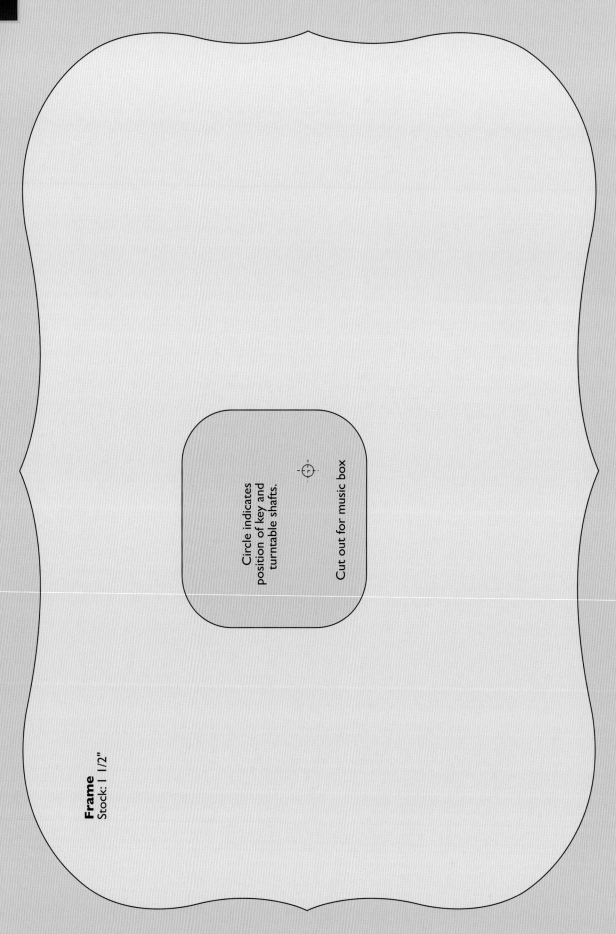

Circle indicates
position of key and
turntable shafts.

Cut out for music box

Frame
Stock: 1 1/2"

Support
Stock: 1/4"

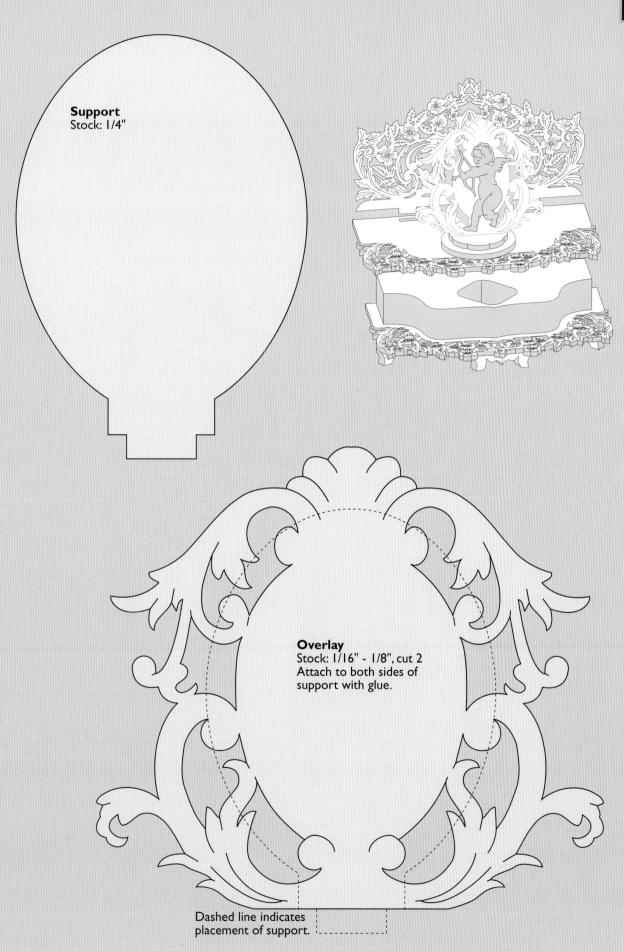

Overlay
Stock: 1/16" - 1/8", cut 2
Attach to both sides of
support with glue.

Dashed line indicates
placement of support.

ROMANCE

Cupid's Aim

Figure
Stock: 1/16" - 1/8", cut 2

Back Crest
Stock: 1/4"

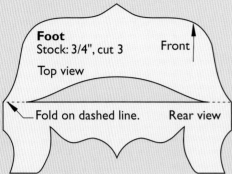

Foot
Stock: 3/4", cut 3

Front

Top view

Fold on dashed line. Rear view

Turntable Overlay
Stock: 1/4"

Overlay

Overlay

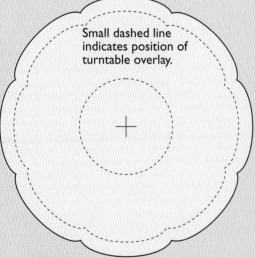

Small dashed line
indicates position of
turntable overlay.

Turntable
Stock: 1/4"
Countersink the bottomside with a
1" Forstner bit 1/16" deep. Secure
the metal turntable with glue or
silicone.

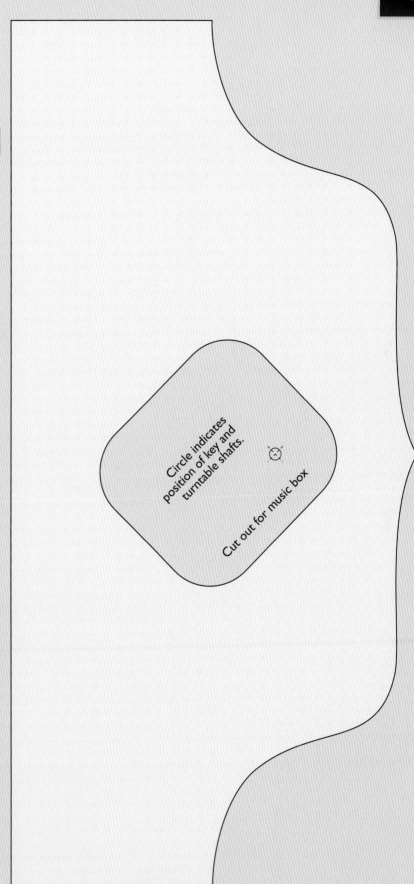

Circle indicates
position of key and
turntable shafts.

Cut out for music box

ROMANCE

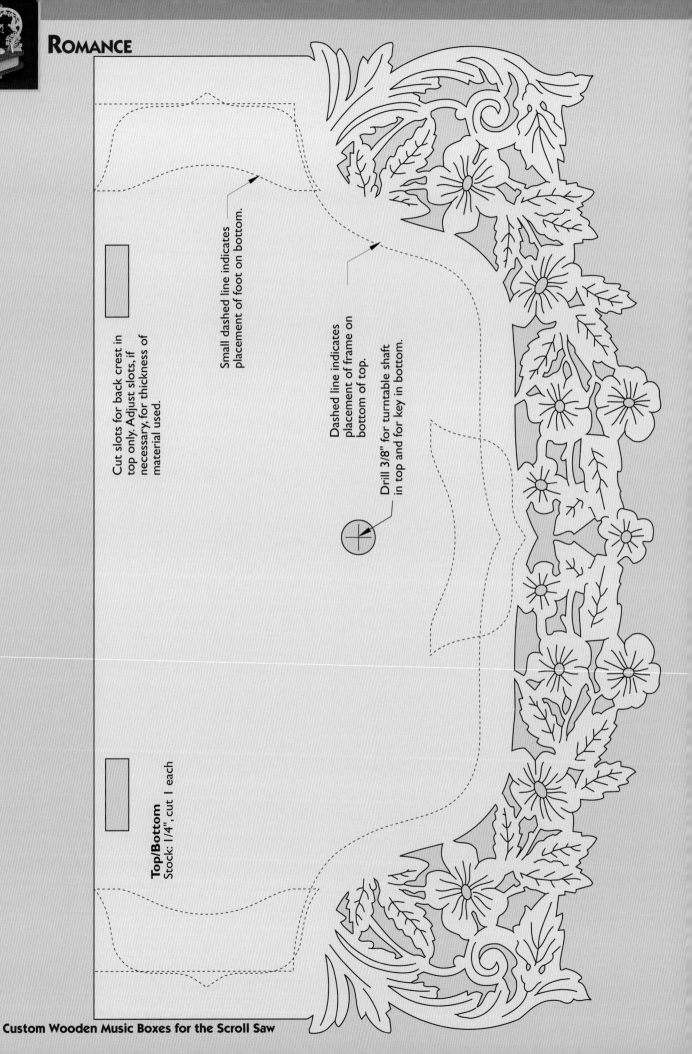

Cut slots for back crest in top only. Adjust slots, if necessary, for thickness of material used.

Small dashed line indicates placement of foot on bottom.

Dashed line indicates placement of frame on bottom of top.

Drill 3/8" for turntable shaft in top and for key in bottom.

Top/Bottom
Stock: 1/4", cut 1 each

Courtship

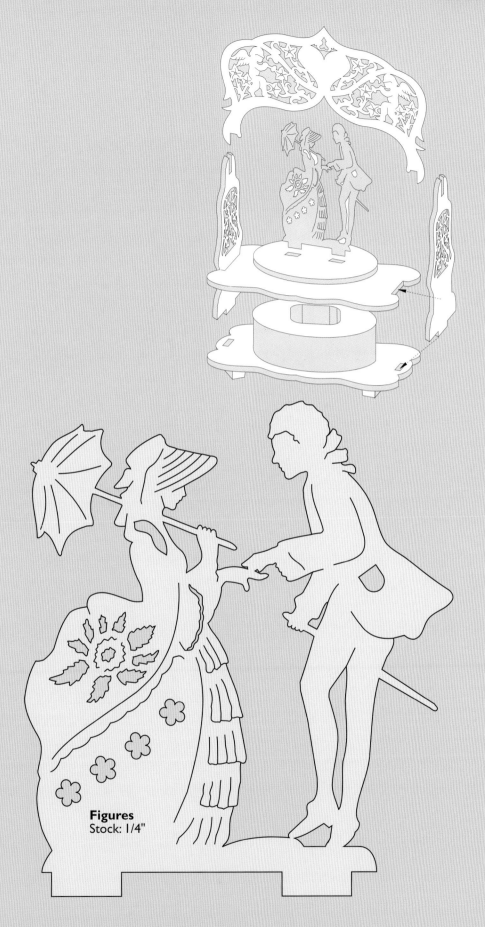

Figures
Stock: 1/4"

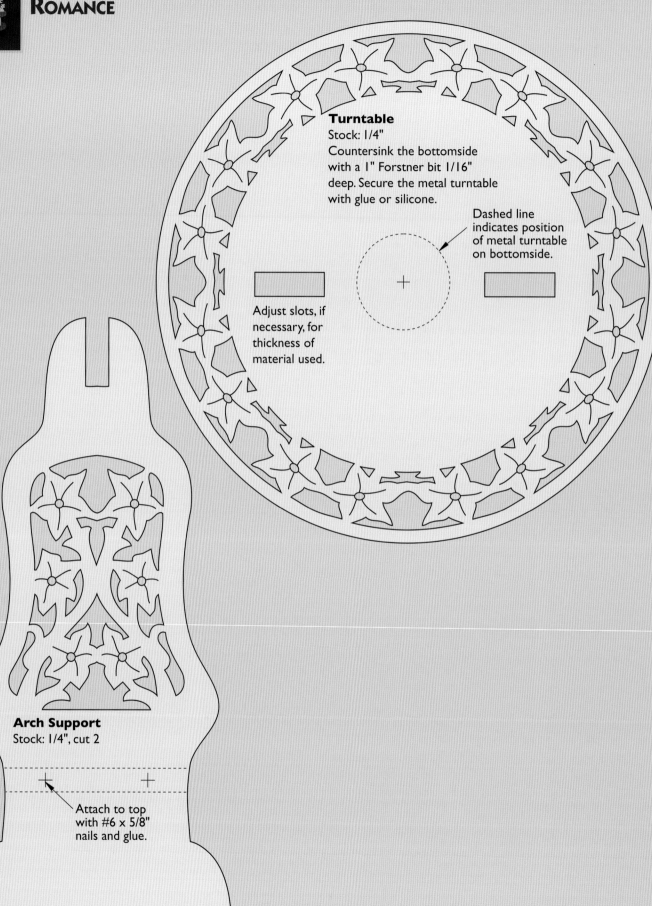

Turntable
Stock: 1/4"
Countersink the bottomside
with a 1" Forstner bit 1/16"
deep. Secure the metal turntable
with glue or silicone.

Dashed line
indicates position
of metal turntable
on bottomside.

Adjust slots, if
necessary, for
thickness of
material used.

Arch Support
Stock: 1/4", cut 2

Attach to top
with #6 x 5/8"
nails and glue.

Courtship

Courtship

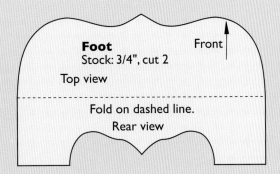

Foot
Stock: 3/4", cut 2

Top view

Front

Fold on dashed line.

Rear view

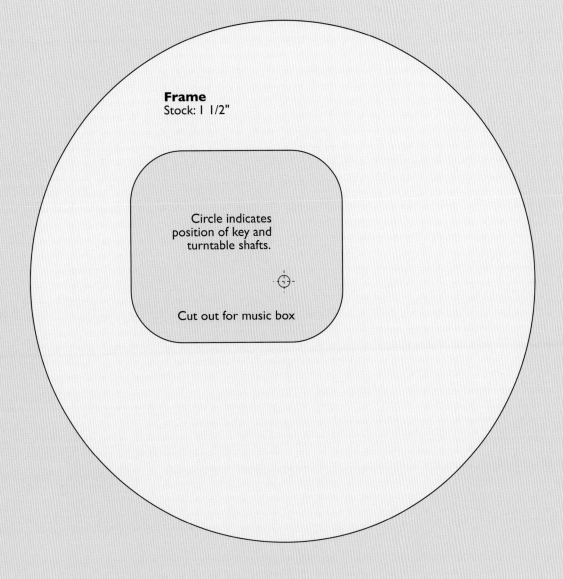

Frame
Stock: 1 1/2"

Circle indicates position of key and turntable shafts.

Cut out for music box

Arch
Stock: 1/4"

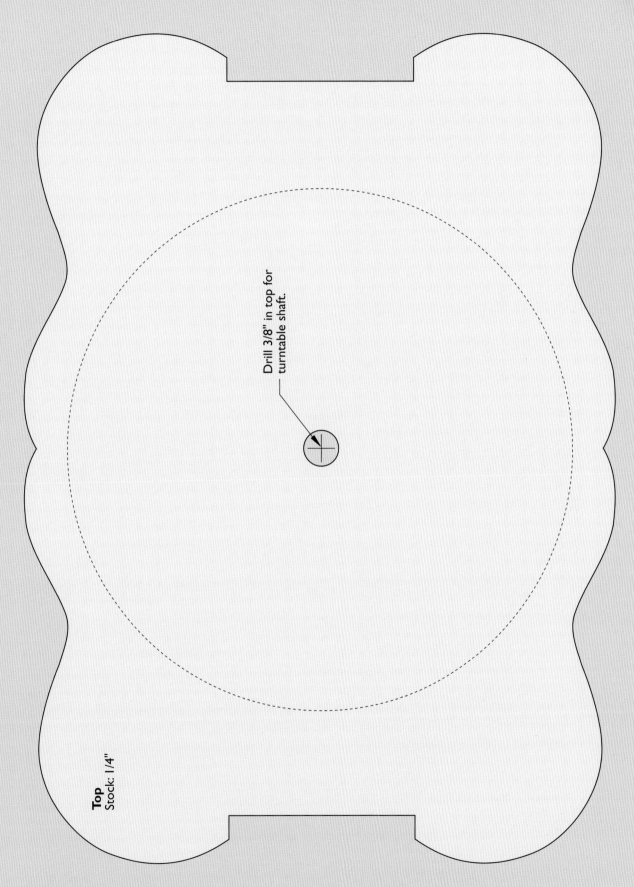

Drill 3/8" in top for turntable shaft.

Top
Stock: 1/4"

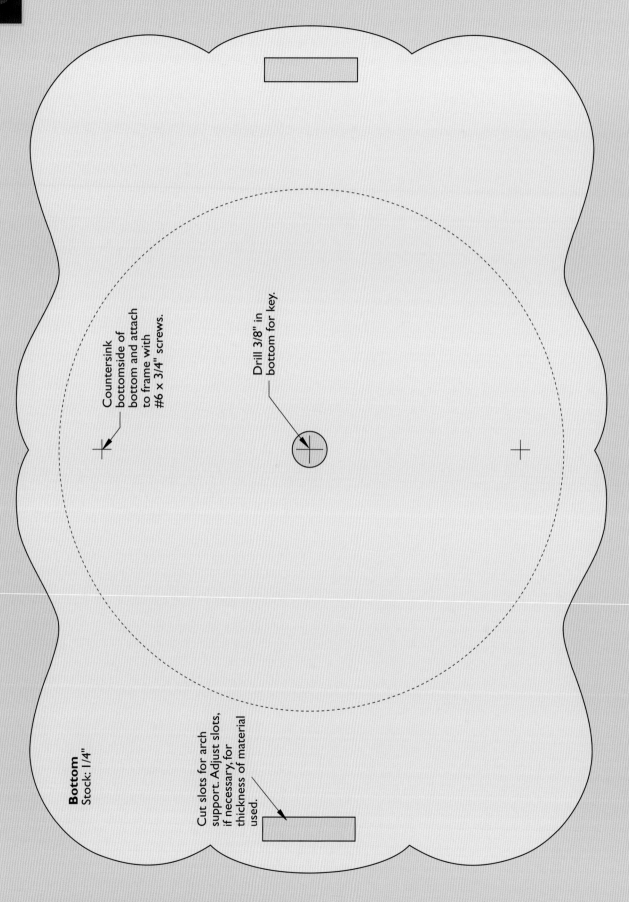

Countersink bottomside of bottom and attach to frame with #6 x 3/4" screws.

Drill 3/8" in bottom for key.

Bottom
Stock: 1/4"

Cut slots for arch support. Adjust slots, if necessary, for thickness of material used.

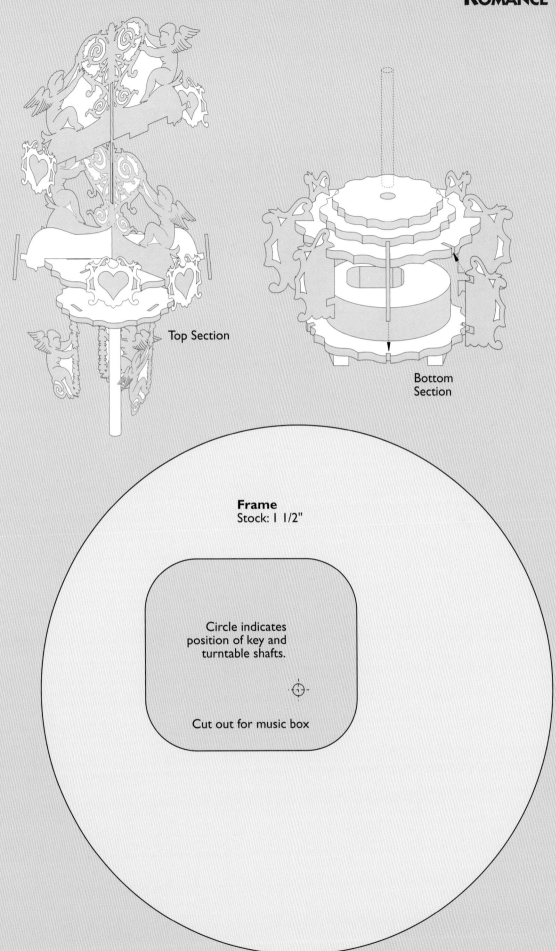

Top Section

Bottom
Section

Frame
Stock: 1 1/2"

Circle indicates
position of key and
turntable shafts.

Cut out for music box

Love's Labor

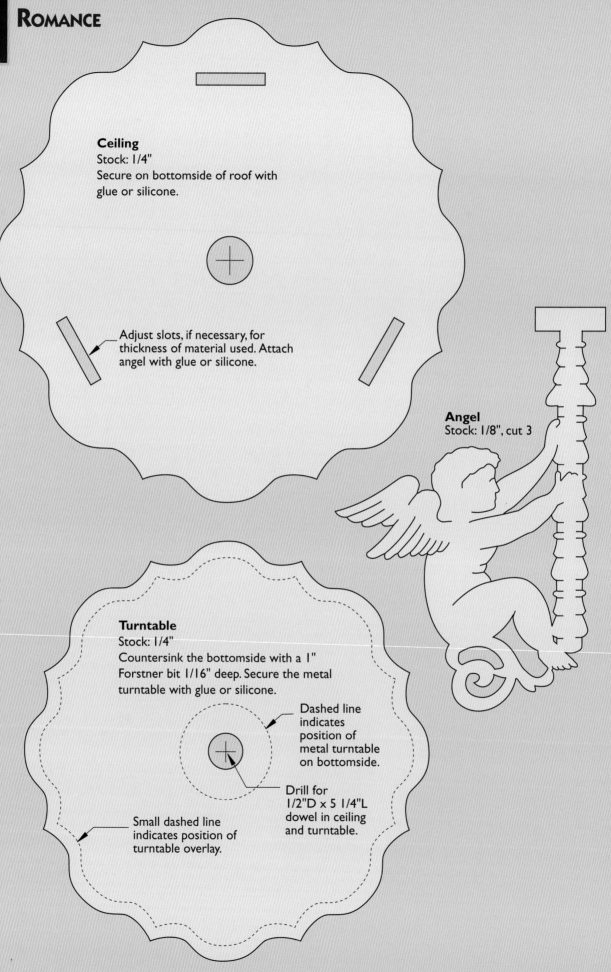

Ceiling
Stock: 1/4"
Secure on bottomside of roof with glue or silicone.

Adjust slots, if necessary, for thickness of material used. Attach angel with glue or silicone.

Angel
Stock: 1/8", cut 3

Turntable
Stock: 1/4"
Countersink the bottomside with a 1" Forstner bit 1/16" deep. Secure the metal turntable with glue or silicone.

Dashed line indicates position of metal turntable on bottomside.

Drill for 1/2"D x 5 1/4"L dowel in ceiling and turntable.

Small dashed line indicates position of turntable overlay.

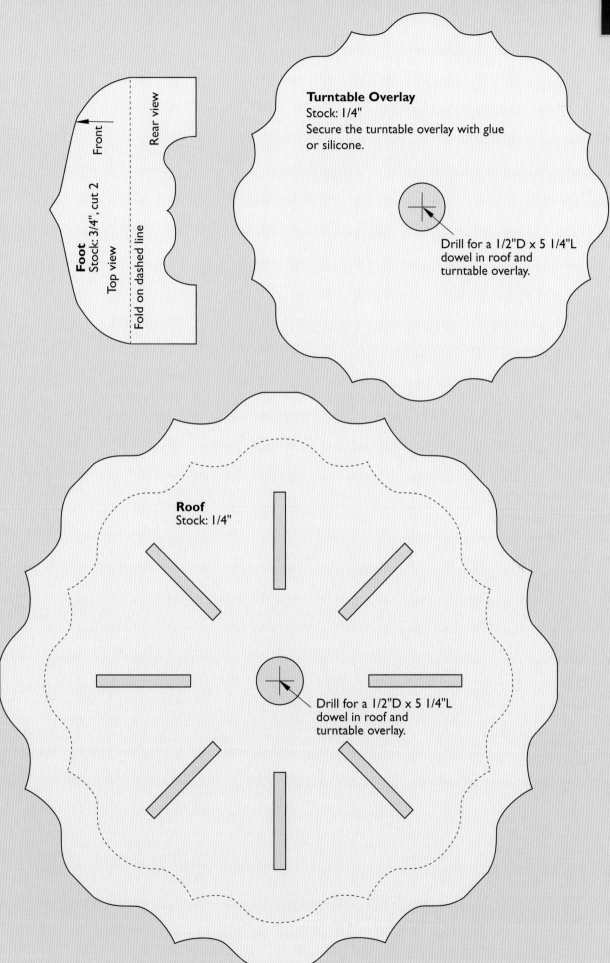

Foot
Stock: 3/4", cut 2

Front

Rear view

Top view

Fold on dashed line

Turntable Overlay
Stock: 1/4"
Secure the turntable overlay with glue or silicone.

Drill for a 1/2"D x 5 1/4"L dowel in roof and turntable overlay.

Roof
Stock: 1/4"

Drill for a 1/2"D x 5 1/4"L dowel in roof and turntable overlay.

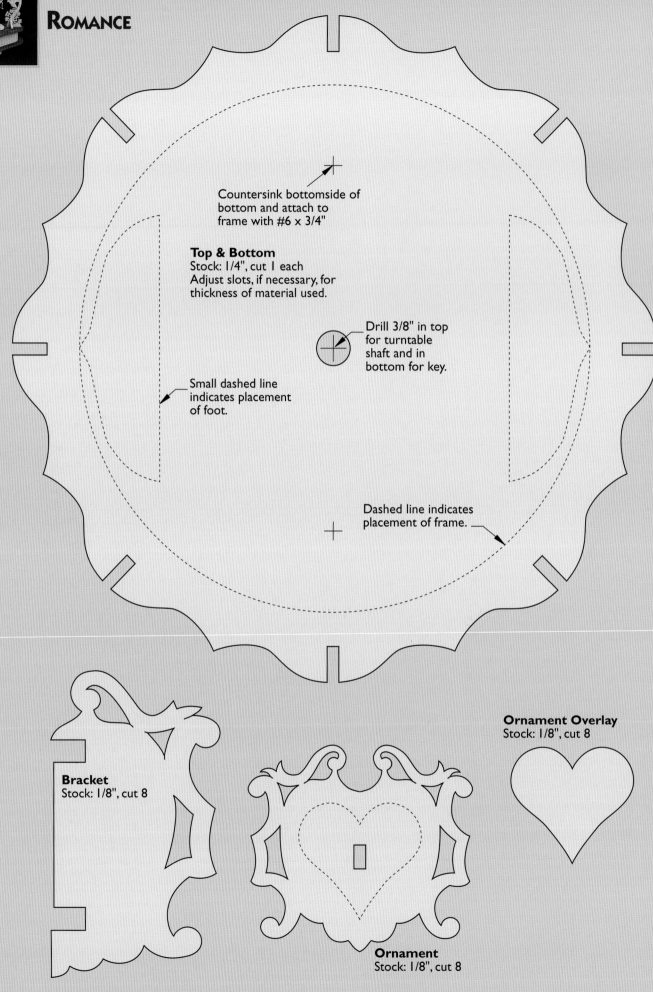

Countersink bottomside of bottom and attach to frame with #6 x 3/4"

Top & Bottom
Stock: 1/4", cut 1 each
Adjust slots, if necessary, for thickness of material used.

Drill 3/8" in top for turntable shaft and in bottom for key.

Small dashed line indicates placement of foot.

Dashed line indicates placement of frame.

Bracket
Stock: 1/8", cut 8

Ornament Overlay
Stock: 1/8", cut 8

Ornament
Stock: 1/8", cut 8

Love's Labor

22.5°   Sand inside edges 22.5° to fit in corner of crest (A) & (B) on roof.

Top view   22.5°

Crest Divider
Stock: 1/8", cut 4

Cut this slot for crest (A)

A

Cut this slot for crest (B)

B

Crest (A) & (B)
Stock: 1/8", cut 1 each

Assembly Instructions

Assemble by first attaching the feet to the bottom with glue or silicone. Next, attach the frame, making sure the music box movement is secure in place. Place the top into position on the frame, being sure all of the slots for the brackets line up before securing it in place. Then, secure the brackets in place. Now, attach the turntable overlay to the turntable, and secure the metal turntable to the bottom of the turntable. Next, secure the ceiling to the bottom of the roof. Then, insert the dowel until it is flush with the top of the roof and glue in place. Secure both crest (B) and (A) into place on the roof, and then add the crest dividers. Secure the angels into place in the ceiling, and the ornament overlays and ornaments on the tabs of the crest and crest dividers. Secure the dowel into the turntable assembly, and attach the metal turntable to the movement.

ROMANCE

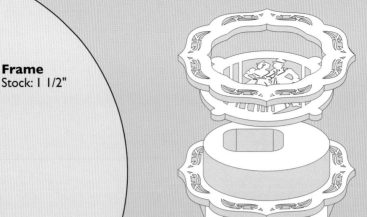

Frame
Stock: 1 1/2"

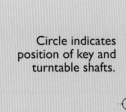

Circle indicates position of key and turntable shafts.

Cut out for music box

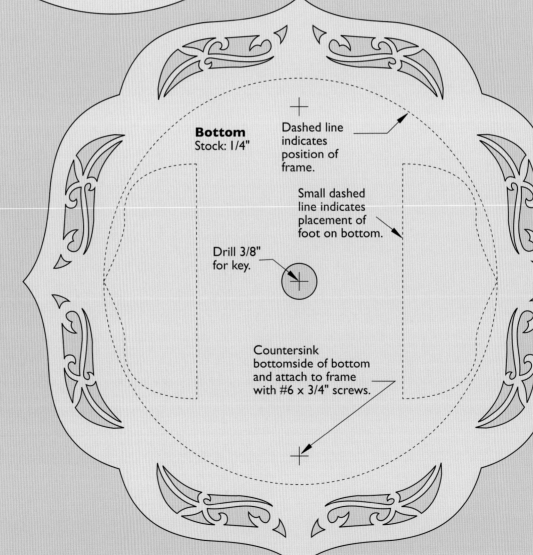

Bottom
Stock: 1/4"

Dashed line indicates position of frame.

Small dashed line indicates placement of foot on bottom.

Drill 3/8" for key.

Countersink bottomside of bottom and attach to frame with #6 x 3/4" screws.

Newlyweds

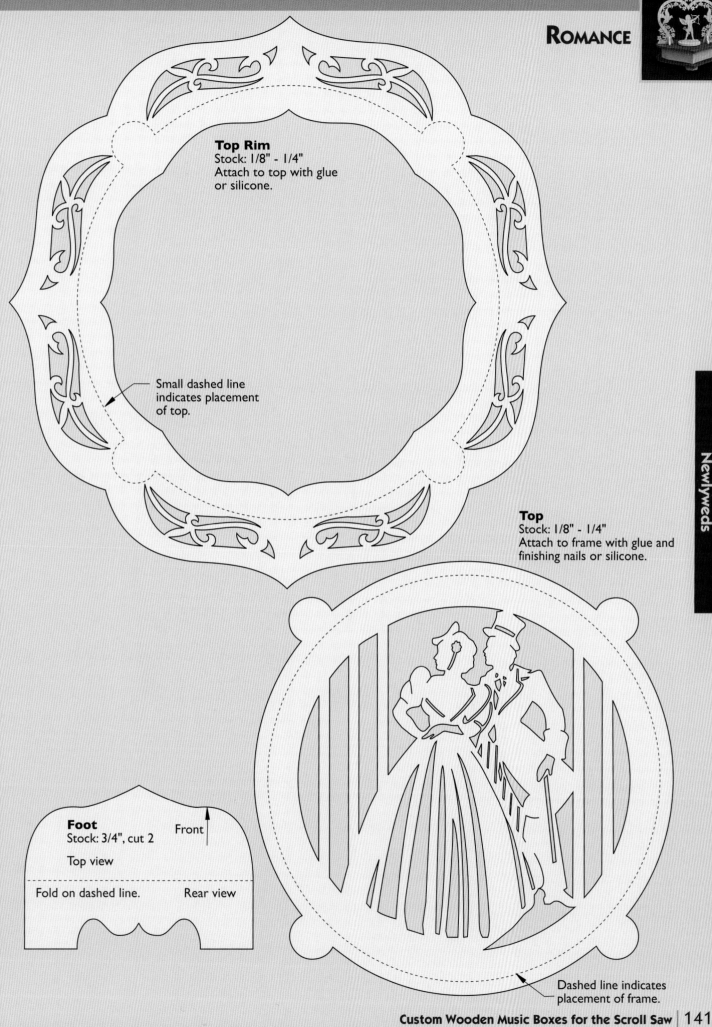

Top Rim
Stock: 1/8" - 1/4"
Attach to top with glue
or silicone.

Small dashed line
indicates placement
of top.

Top
Stock: 1/8" - 1/4"
Attach to frame with glue and
finishing nails or silicone.

Foot
Stock: 3/4", cut 2

Front

Top view

Fold on dashed line.   Rear view

Dashed line indicates
placement of frame.

Newlyweds

ROMANCE

Forever

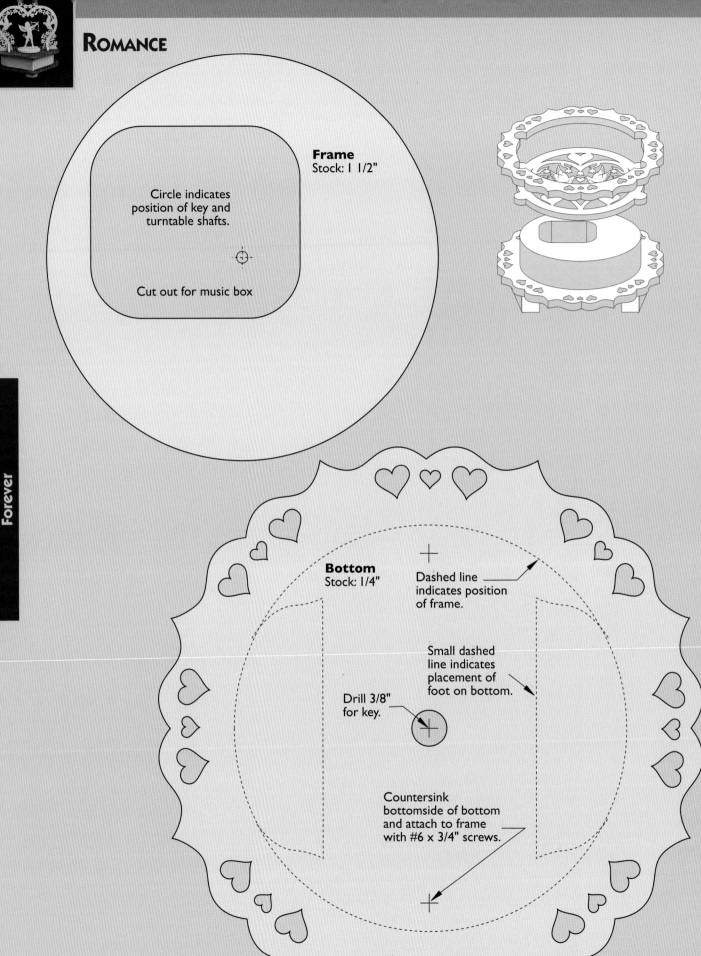

Frame
Stock: 1 1/2"

Circle indicates position of key and turntable shafts.

Cut out for music box

Bottom
Stock: 1/4"

Dashed line indicates position of frame.

Small dashed line indicates placement of foot on bottom.

Drill 3/8" for key.

Countersink bottomside of bottom and attach to frame with #6 x 3/4" screws.

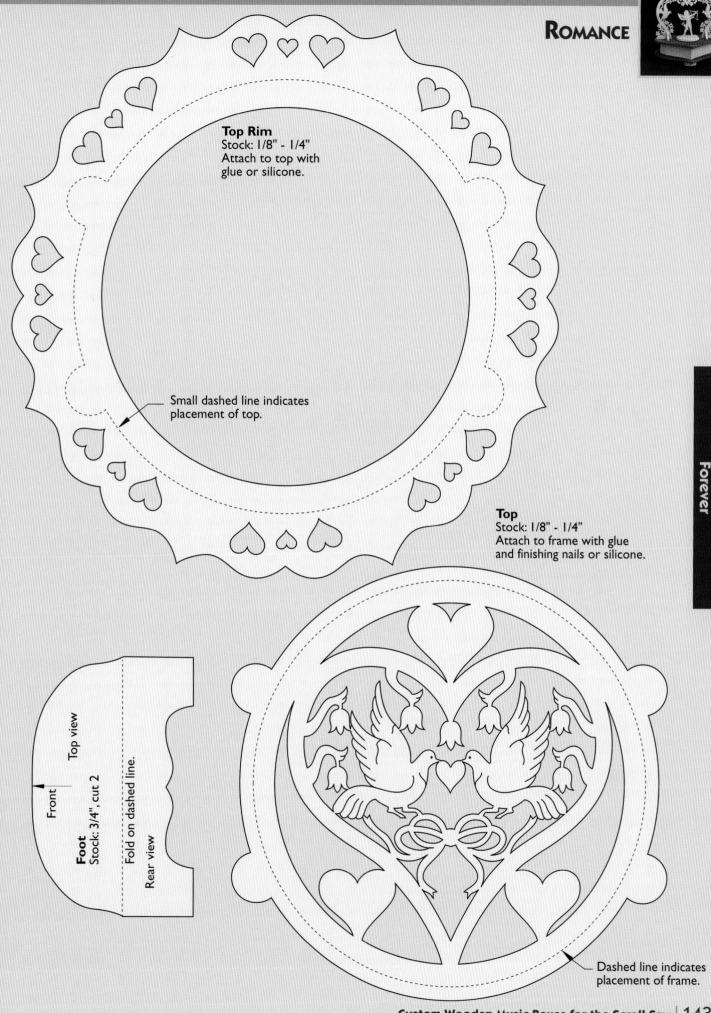

Top Rim
Stock: 1/8" - 1/4"
Attach to top with
glue or silicone.

Small dashed line indicates
placement of top.

Top
Stock: 1/8" - 1/4"
Attach to frame with glue
and finishing nails or silicone.

Forever

Top view

Front

Foot
Stock: 3/4", cut 2

Fold on dashed line.

Rear view

Dashed line indicates
placement of frame.

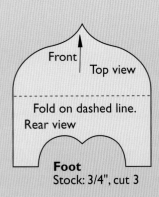

ROMANCE

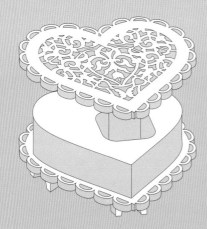

Front

Top view

Fold on dashed line.
Rear view

Foot
Stock: 3/4", cut 3

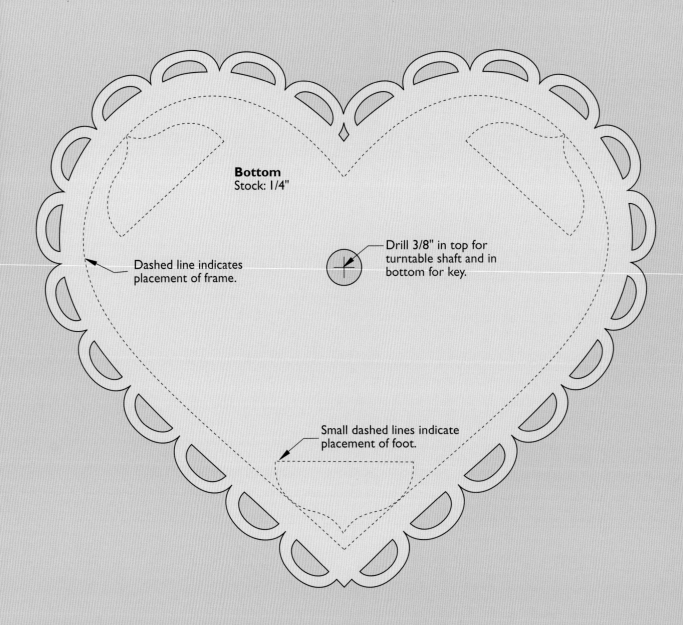

Bottom
Stock: 1/4"

Dashed line indicates
placement of frame.

Drill 3/8" in top for
turntable shaft and in
bottom for key.

Small dashed lines indicate
placement of foot.

Frame
Stock: 1 1/2"

Cut out for music box

Circle indicates
position of key and
turntable shafts.

Top
Stock: 1/4"

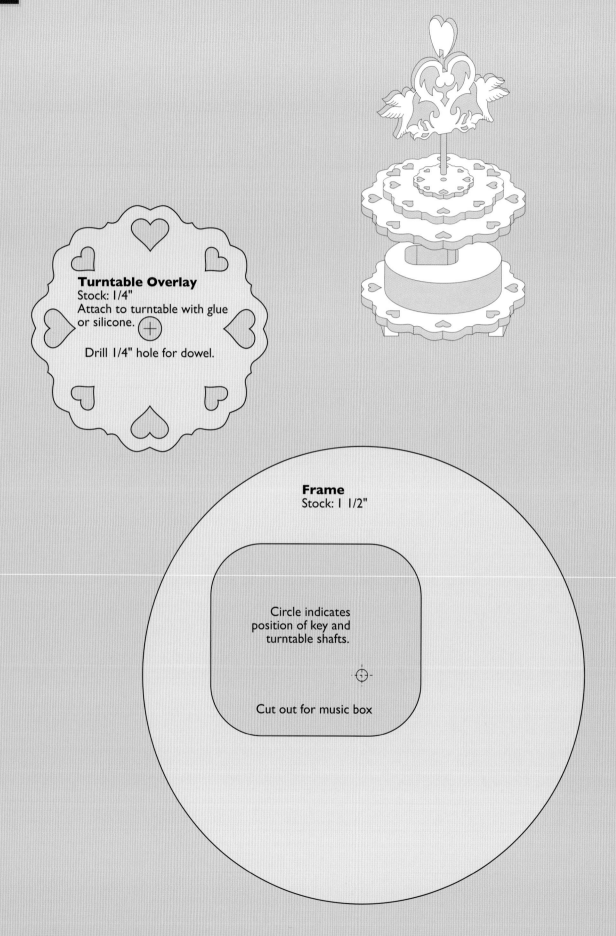

Turntable Overlay
Stock: 1/4"
Attach to turntable with glue
or silicone.

Drill 1/4" hole for dowel.

Frame
Stock: 1 1/2"

Circle indicates
position of key and
turntable shafts.

Cut out for music box

Love Birds

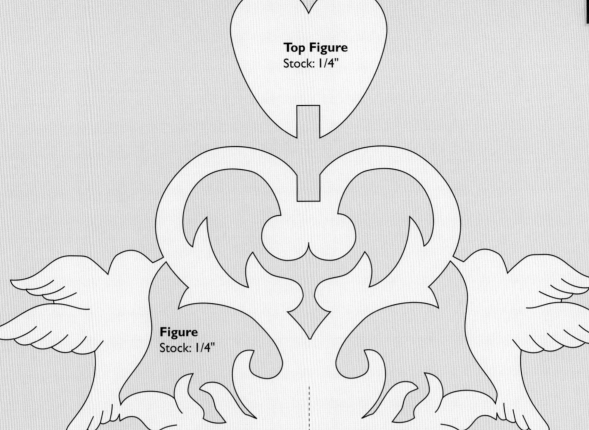

Top Figure
Stock: 1/4"

Figure
Stock: 1/4"

Drill for a 1/4"D x 3 1/2"L dowel. Secure
in figure and turntable with glue.

Turntable
Stock: 1/4"
Countersink the bottomside with a
1" Forstner bit 1/16" deep. Secure the
metal turntable with glue or silicone.

Small dashed line
indicates position
of metal turntable
on bottomside.

Dashed line
indicates position of
turntable overlay.

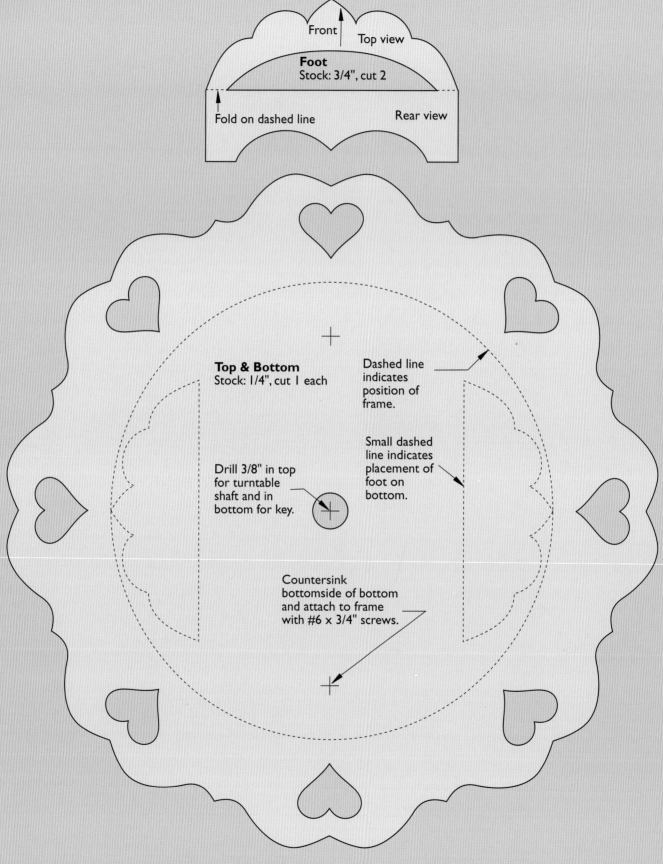

Front Top view

Foot
Stock: 3/4", cut 2

Fold on dashed line Rear view

Top & Bottom
Stock: 1/4", cut 1 each

Dashed line
indicates
position of
frame.

Small dashed
line indicates
placement of
foot on
bottom.

Drill 3/8" in top
for turntable
shaft and in
bottom for key.

Countersink
bottomside of bottom
and attach to frame
with #6 x 3/4" screws.

VICTORIAN

Side Support
Stock: 1/4", cut 6

30°   Top view   30°

Side
Stock: 1/4", cut 6

Note: Because copy machines are not 100% accurate, you may need to adjust the width.

Assembly Instructions

Assemble by first attaching one side support and one side to the bottom. Continue in a clockwise direction with the remaining side supports and sides. Next, secure the top into position. Now, attach the lid underlay to the bottom of the lid. Then, secure the handles, handle support, overlay, and top overlay into position.

Note: Most copy machines are not 100% accurate, which can result in distortion of your pattern pieces. Since this project has several slots and tab connections, it may be necessary to adjust them for an accurate fit.

Top
Stock: 1/4"

Lid Underlay
Stock: 1/4"
Note: After cutting the interior section, use it as the lid underlay. Cut or sand slightly smaller before securing to the bottom of the lid. This will help the lid fit easier into position.

Use #60 drill bit to start cut for lid underlay.

Keepsake

Victorian

Top Overlay
Stock: 1/8"
Attach to overlay with glue.

Drill for finial or brass knob of your choice.

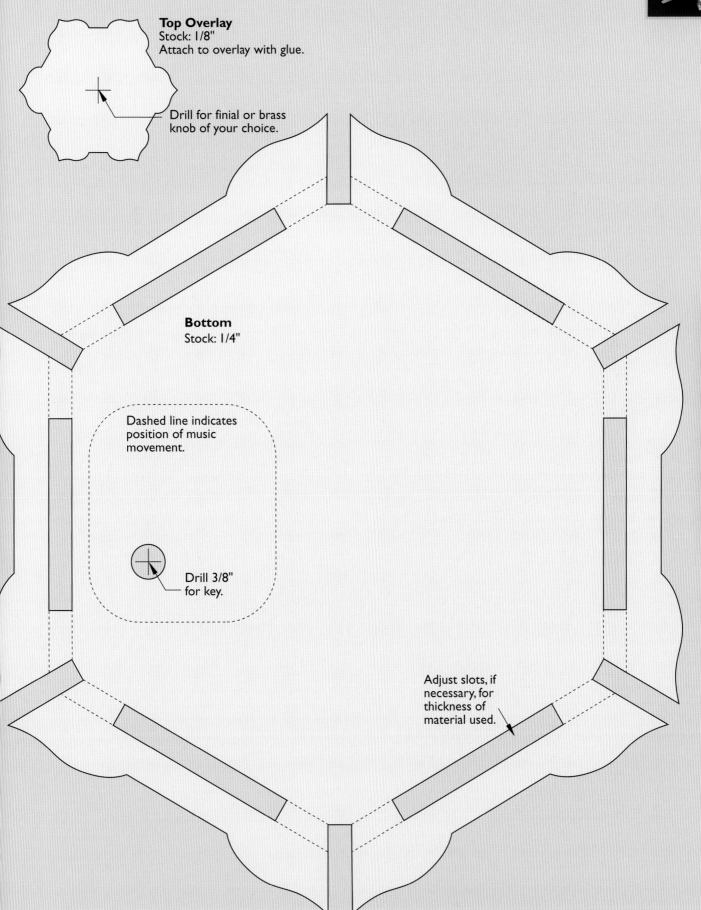

Bottom
Stock: 1/4"

Dashed line indicates position of music movement.

Drill 3/8" for key.

Adjust slots, if necessary, for thickness of material used.

Keepsake

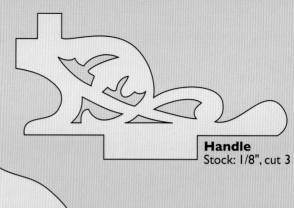

Overlay
Stock: 1/8"

Handle Support
Stock: 1/4"

Handle
Stock: 1/8", cut 3

Lid
Stock: 1/4"

Dashed line indicates
placement of lid
underlay.

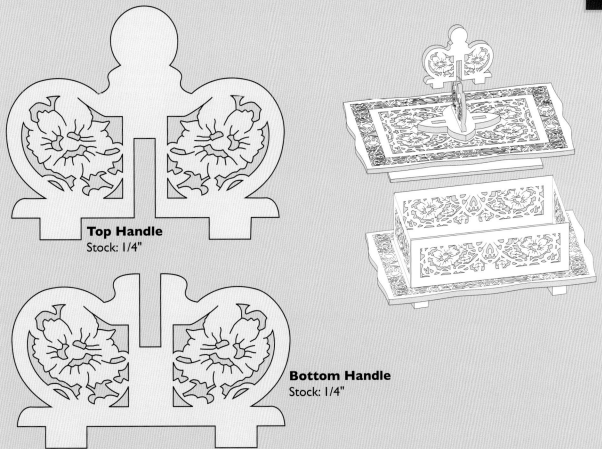

Top Handle
Stock: 1/4"

Bottom Handle
Stock: 1/4"

Side
Stock: 1/4", cut 2

Attach to end with glue
and finishing nails.

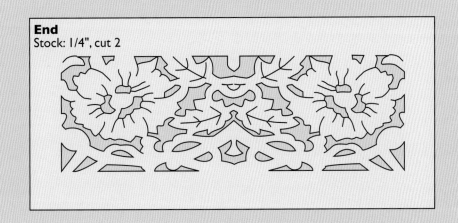

End
Stock: 1/4", cut 2

Lid Support
Stock: 1/8"
Attach to bottomside of
lid with glue or silicone.

Foot
Stock: 3/4", cut 4

Front

Top view

Fold on dashed line.

Rear view

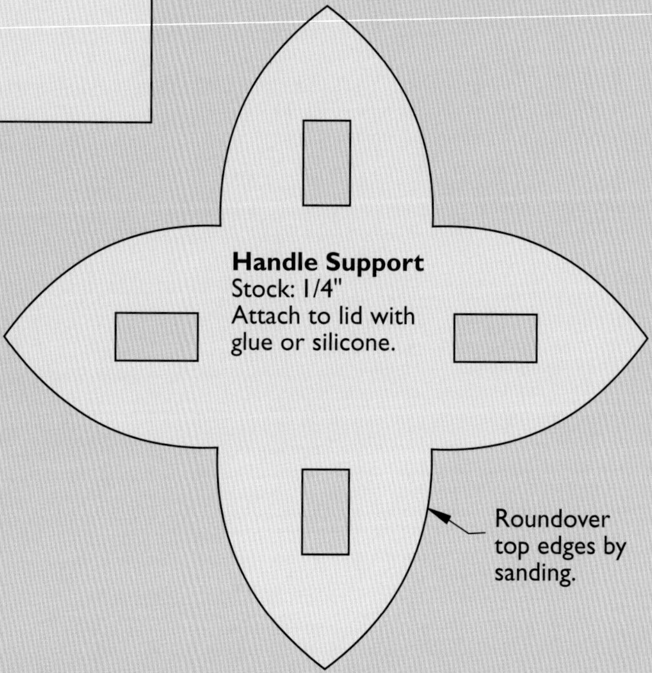

Handle Support
Stock: 1/4"
Attach to lid with
glue or silicone.

Roundover
top edges by
sanding.

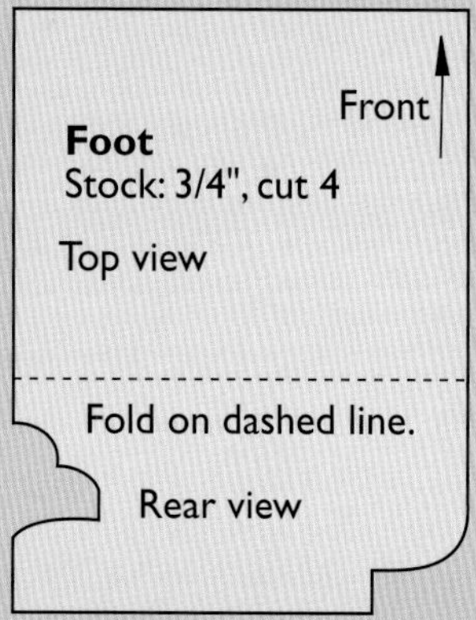

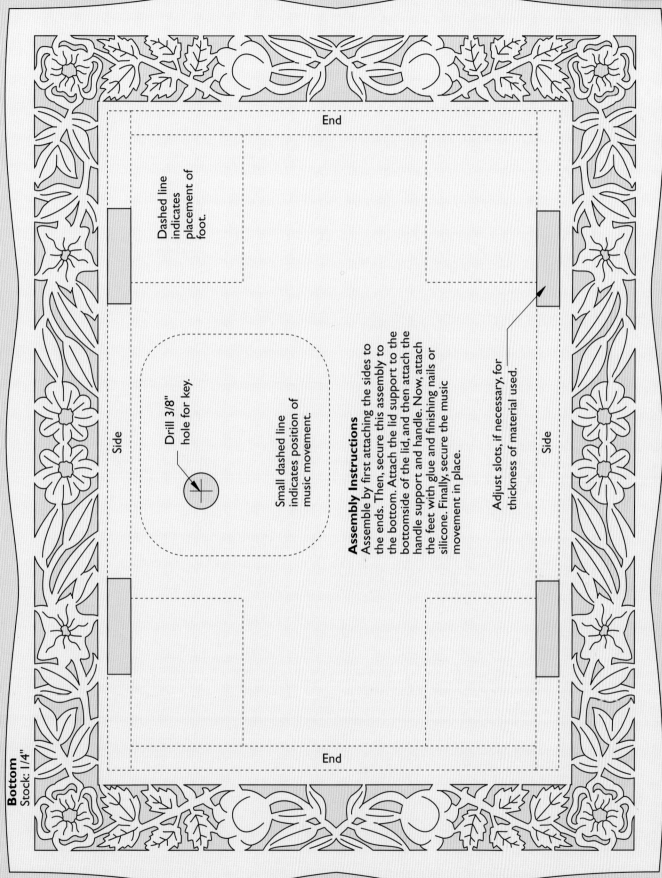

Bottom
Stock: 1/4"

Side

End

Dashed line indicates placement of foot.

Drill 3/8" hole for key.

Small dashed line indicates position of music movement.

Assembly Instructions

Assemble by first attaching the sides to the ends. Then, secure this assembly to the bottom. Attach the lid support to the bottomside of the lid, and then attach the handle support and handle. Now, attach the feet with glue and finishing nails or silicone. Finally, secure the music movement in place.

Adjust slots, if necessary, for thickness of material used.

Side

End

VICTORIAN

Elegance

End

Side

Side

End

Small dashed line indicates placement of handle support.

Lid
Stock: 1/4"

Pinnacle #2
Stock: 1/4"

Pinnacle #1
Stock: 1/4"

Roof
Stock: 1/4"

Serenity Dove

Dashed line indicates
placement of frame.

Top & Bottom
Stock: 1/4", cut 1 each
Cut slots in top only.

Drill 3/8" in
top for
turntable shaft
and in bottom
for key.

Small dashed
line indicates
placement of foot.

Foot
Stock: 3/4", cut 3   Front

Top view

Fold on dashed line.

Rear view

1   Top
     3/4"

2 Rear
   view
      Back
   1 3/16"

3   Top view
         Top

Figure
Stock: 1/4"

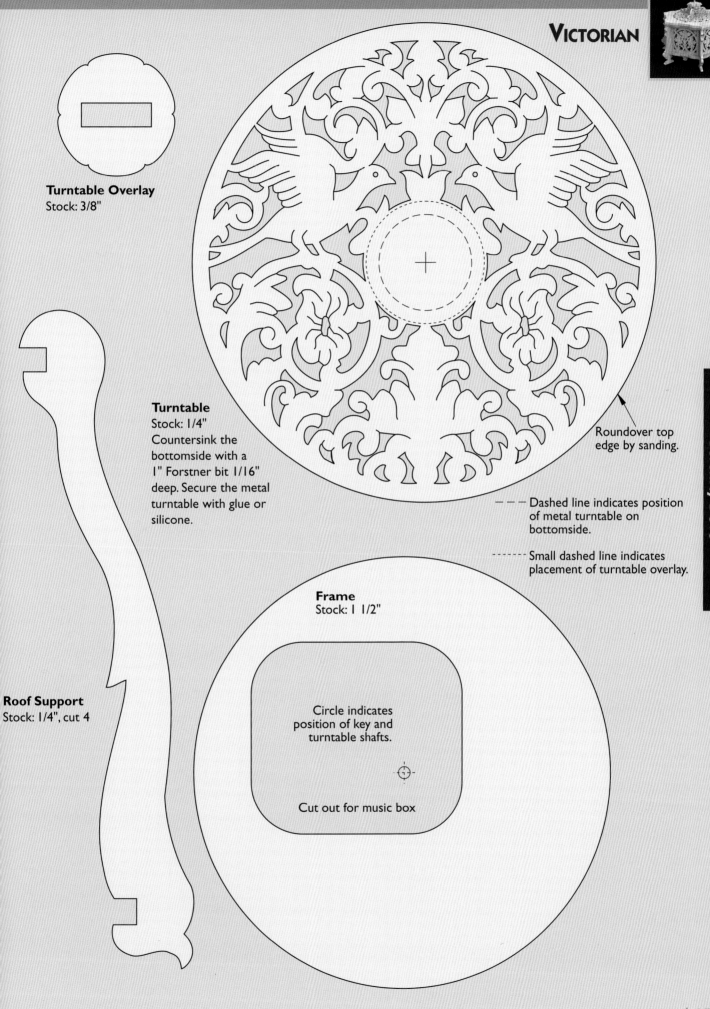

Turntable Overlay
Stock: 3/8"

Turntable
Stock: 1/4"
Countersink the
bottomside with a
1" Forstner bit 1/16"
deep. Secure the metal
turntable with glue or
silicone.

Roundover top
edge by sanding.

– – – Dashed line indicates position
of metal turntable on
bottomside.

- - - - - - - Small dashed line indicates
placement of turntable overlay.

Roof Support
Stock: 1/4", cut 4

Frame
Stock: 1 1/2"

Circle indicates
position of key and
turntable shafts.

Cut out for music box

VICTORIAN

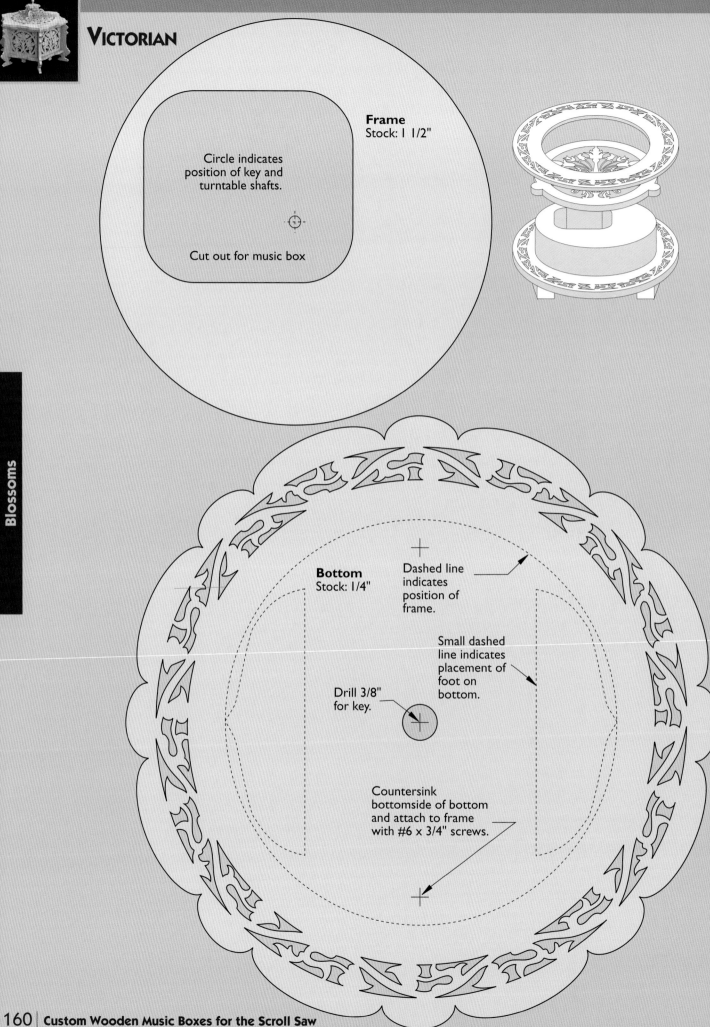

Frame
Stock: 1 1/2"

Circle indicates
position of key and
turntable shafts.

Cut out for music box

Bottom
Stock: 1/4"

Dashed line
indicates
position of
frame.

Small dashed
line indicates
placement of
foot on
bottom.

Drill 3/8"
for key.

Countersink
bottomside of bottom
and attach to frame
with #6 x 3/4" screws.

Blossoms

Top Rim
Stock: 1/8" - 1/4"
Attach to top with
glue or silicone.

Small dashed line
indicates placement
of top.

Top
Stock: 1/8" - 1/4"
Attach to frame with
glue and finishing nails
or silicone.

Foot
Stock: 3/4", cut 2
Top view
Fold on dashed line.
Front
Rear view

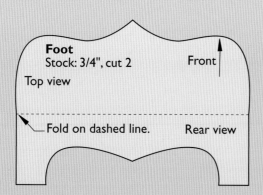

Foot
Stock: 3/4", cut 2

Top view

Front

Fold on dashed line.

Rear view

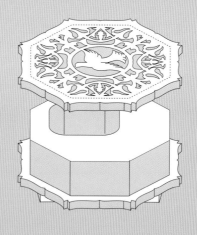

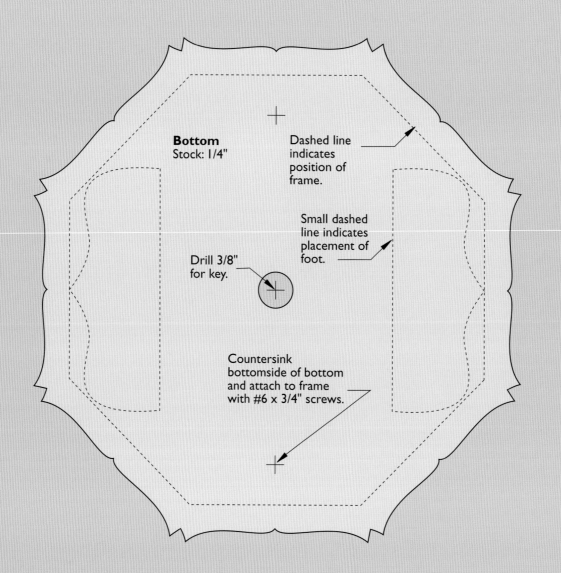

Bottom
Stock: 1/4"

Dashed line
indicates
position of
frame.

Small dashed
line indicates
placement of
foot.

Drill 3/8"
for key.

Countersink
bottomside of bottom
and attach to frame
with #6 x 3/4" screws.

Dove's Wings

Top
Stock: 1/4"

Dove's Wings

Frame
Stock: 1 1/2"

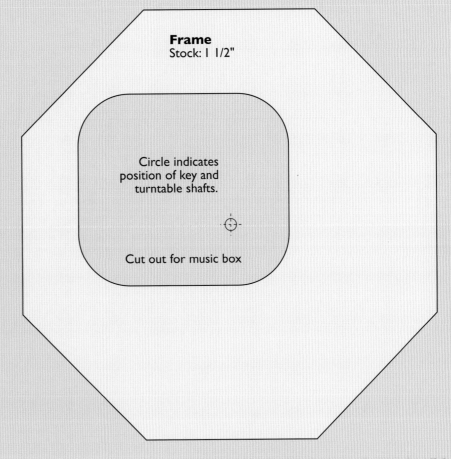

Circle indicates
position of key and
turntable shafts.

Cut out for music box

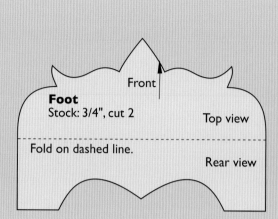

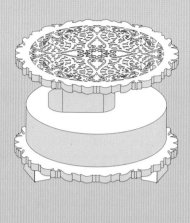

Foot
Stock: 3/4", cut 2

Front

Top view

Fold on dashed line.

Rear view

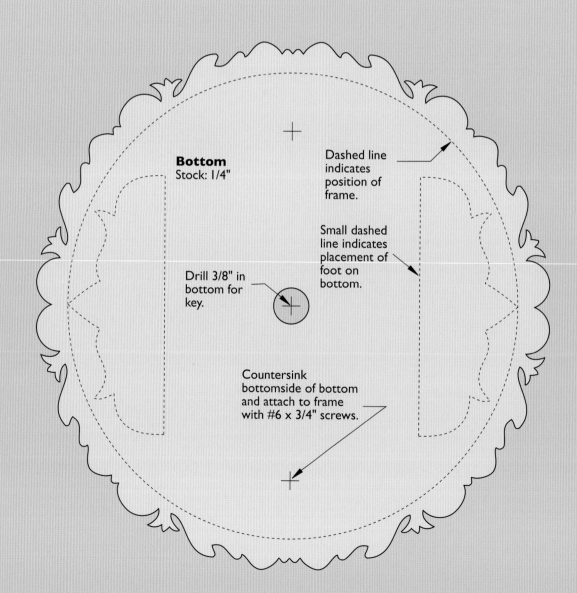

Bottom
Stock: 1/4"

Dashed line indicates position of frame.

Small dashed line indicates placement of foot on bottom.

Drill 3/8" in bottom for key.

Countersink bottomside of bottom and attach to frame with #6 x 3/4" screws.

Lace

Top
Stock: 1/4"

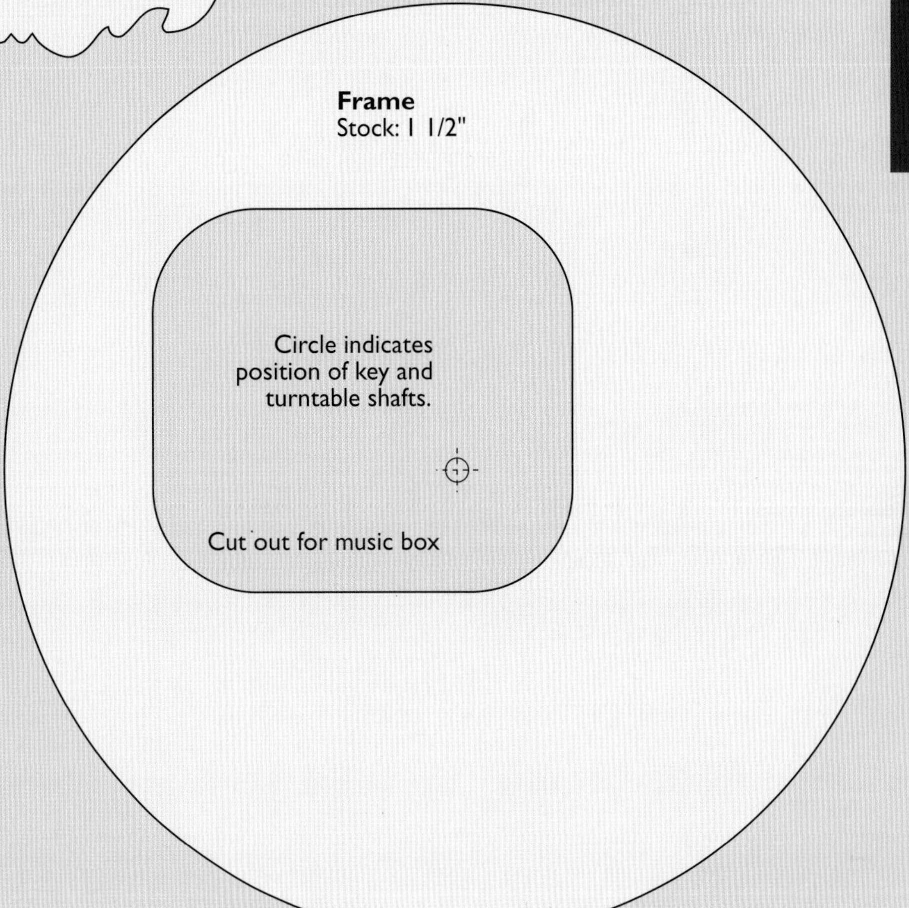

Frame
Stock: 1 1/2"

Circle indicates
position of key and
turntable shafts.

Cut out for music box

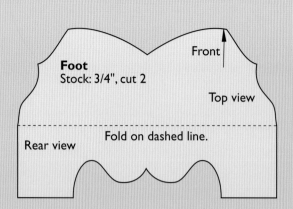

Foot
Stock: 3/4", cut 2

Front

Top view

Rear view   Fold on dashed line.

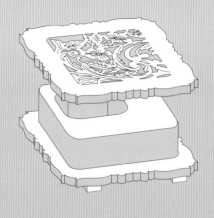

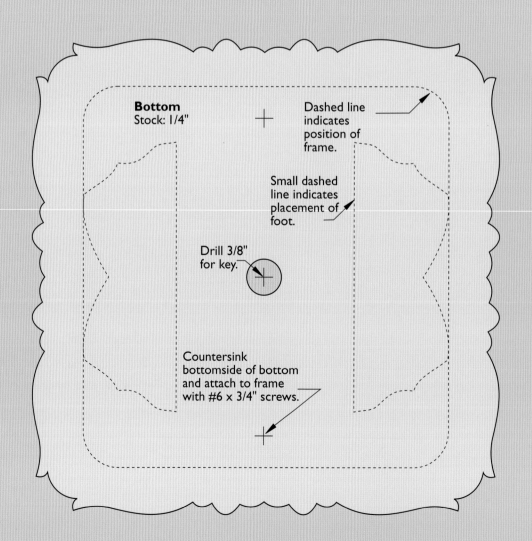

Bottom
Stock: 1/4"

Dashed line indicates position of frame.

Small dashed line indicates placement of foot.

Drill 3/8" for key.

Countersink bottomside of bottom and attach to frame with #6 x 3/4" screws.

Top
Stock: 1/4"

Frame
Stock: 1 1/2"

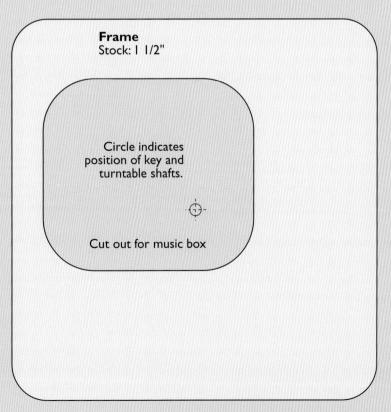

Circle indicates
position of key and
turntable shafts.

Cut out for music box

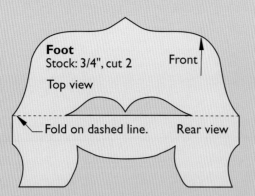

Foot
Stock: 3/4", cut 2

Front

Top view

Fold on dashed line.   Rear view

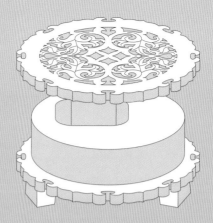

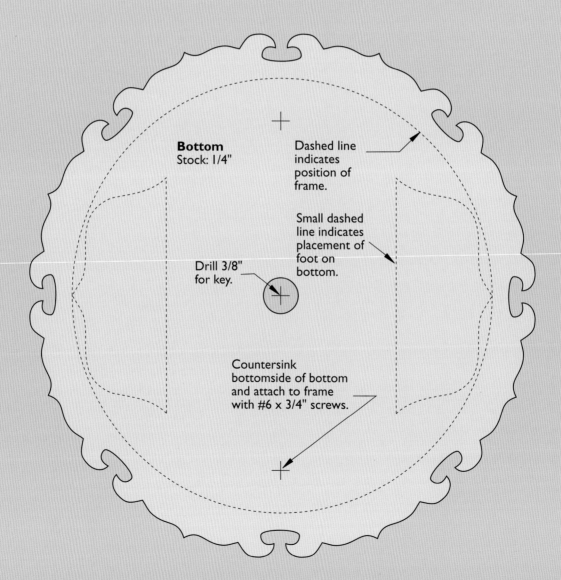

Bottom
Stock: 1/4"

Dashed line indicates position of frame.

Small dashed line indicates placement of foot on bottom.

Drill 3/8" for key.

Countersink bottomside of bottom and attach to frame with #6 x 3/4" screws.

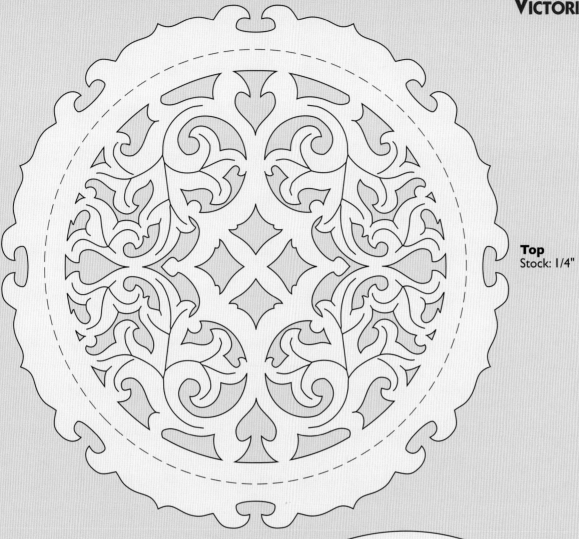

Top
Stock: 1/4"

Frame
Stock: 1 1/2"

Circle indicates
position of key and
turntable shafts.

Cut out for music box

Foot
Stock: 3/4", cut 2

Front

Top view

Fold on dashed line.

Rear view

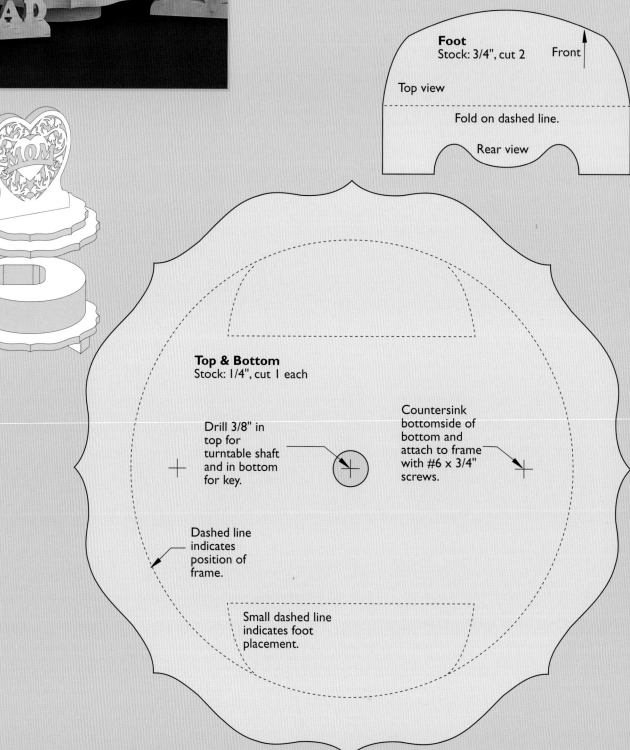

Design 1

Top & Bottom
Stock: 1/4", cut 1 each

Drill 3/8" in
top for
turntable shaft
and in bottom
for key.

Countersink
bottomside of
bottom and
attach to frame
with #6 x 3/4"
screws.

Dashed line
indicates
position of
frame.

Small dashed line
indicates foot
placement.

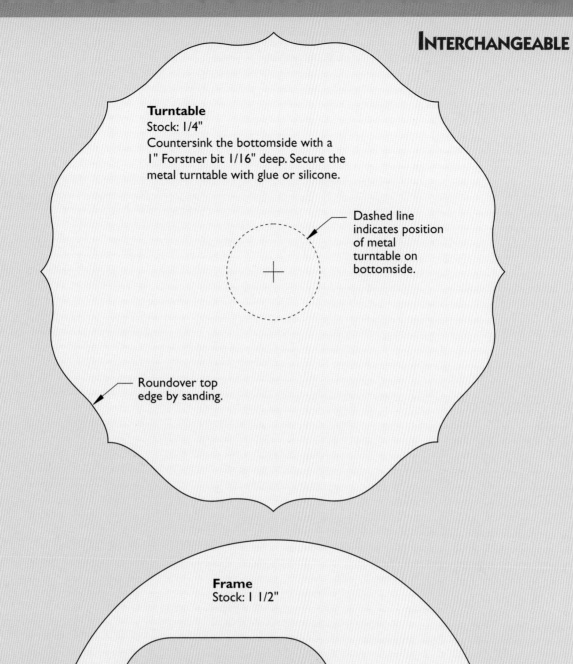

Turntable
Stock: 1/4"
Countersink the bottomside with a 1" Forstner bit 1/16" deep. Secure the metal turntable with glue or silicone.

Dashed line indicates position of metal turntable on bottomside.

Roundover top edge by sanding.

Frame
Stock: 1 1/2"

Circle indicates position of key and turntable shafts.

Cut out for music box

Design 1

Design 1

Snowman
Stock: 3/8"

Tree
Stock: 3/8"

Motorcycle
Stock: 3/8"

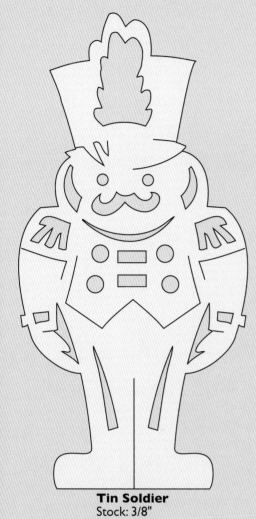

Tin Soldier
Stock: 3/8"

Santa
Stock: 3/8"

Design 1

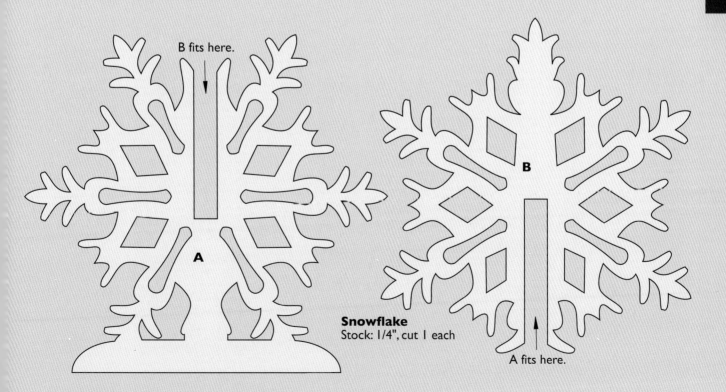

B fits here.

A

B

Snowflake
Stock: 1/4", cut 1 each

A fits here.

Reindeer
Stock: 3/8"

Easter Duck
Stock: 3/8"

B fits here.

A

Snowflake
Stock: 1/4", cut 1 each

B

A fits here.

Elves
Stock: 3/8", cut 1 each
Arrange as desired on
turntable.

Easter Bunny
Stock: 3/8"

Seat & Back
Stock: 1/4", cut 1 each

Back

Sleigh Side
Stock: 1/4", cut 2

Seat

Design 1

Design 1

Mother
Stock: 3/8"

Noel
Stock: 3/8"

NOEL

DAD

Overlay
Stock: 1/16" - 1/8"

MOM

Heart
Stock: 3/8"

Father
Stock: 3/8"

Eagle & Catch
Stock: 3/8"

Easter Chick
Stock: 3/8"

Angel
Stock: 3/8"

Design 1

INTERCHANGEABLE

Design 1

Heart
Stock: 1/16" - 1/4"

Heart / Bouquet Arch
Stock: 3/8"

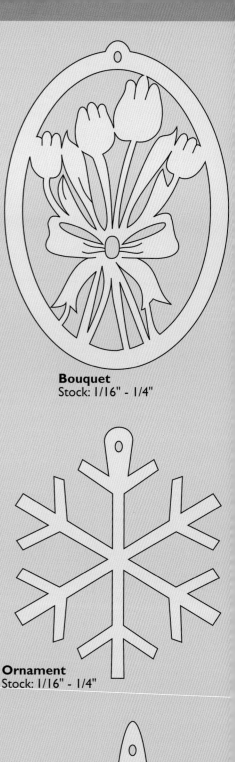

Bouquet
Stock: 1/16" - 1/4"

Ornament
Stock: 1/16" - 1/4"

Ornament
Stock: 1/16" - 1/4"

Ornament Arch
Stock: 3/8"

Ornament
Stock: 1/16" - 1/4"

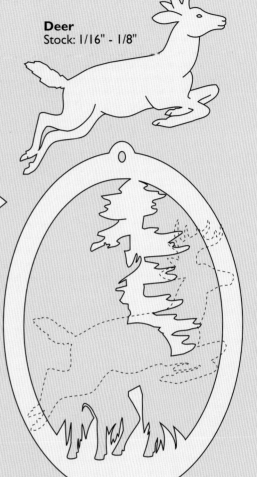

Deer
Stock: 1/16" - 1/8"

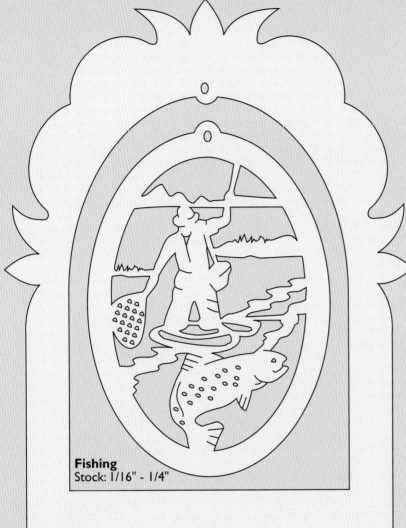

Fishing
Stock: 1/16" - 1/4"

Wildlife Arch
Stock: 3/8"

Tree
Stock: 1/16" - 1/4"
Option: Both deer can be used on one music box, one on each side or a single deer can be used.

Design 1

Ornament
Stock: 1/16" - 1/4"

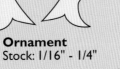

Ornament
Stock: 1/16" - 1/4"

Deer
Stock: 1/16" - 1/8"

Easter Eggs
Stock: 1/16" - 1/4"

Flowers
Stock: 1/16" - 1/4"

Easter / Spring Arch
Stock: 3/8"

Easter Bunny
Stock: 3/8"

Cross
Stock: 1/16" - 1/4"

Design 1

Foot
Stock: 3/4", cut 2   Front

Top view

Fold on dashed line.

Rear view

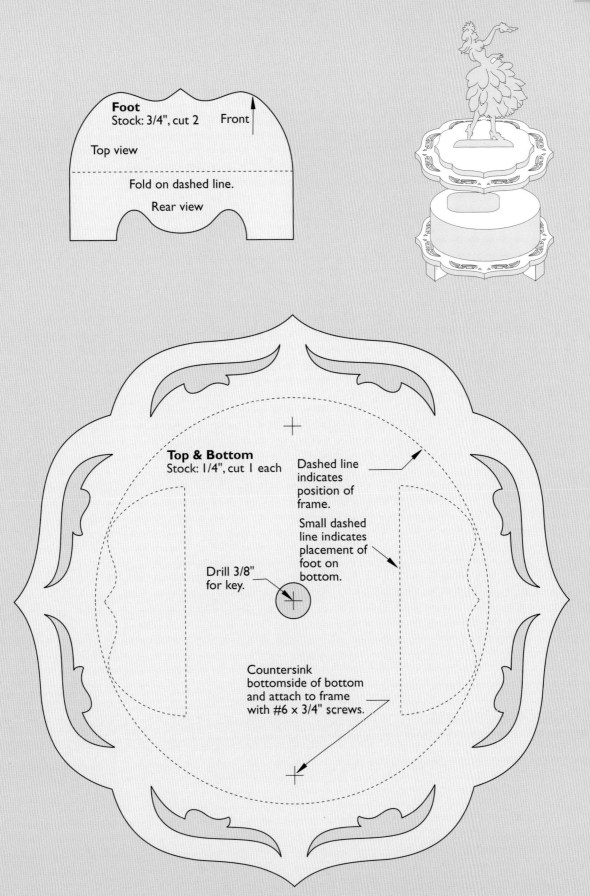

Top & Bottom
Stock: 1/4", cut 1 each

Dashed line indicates position of frame.

Small dashed line indicates placement of foot on bottom.

Drill 3/8" for key.

Countersink bottomside of bottom and attach to frame with #6 x 3/4" screws.

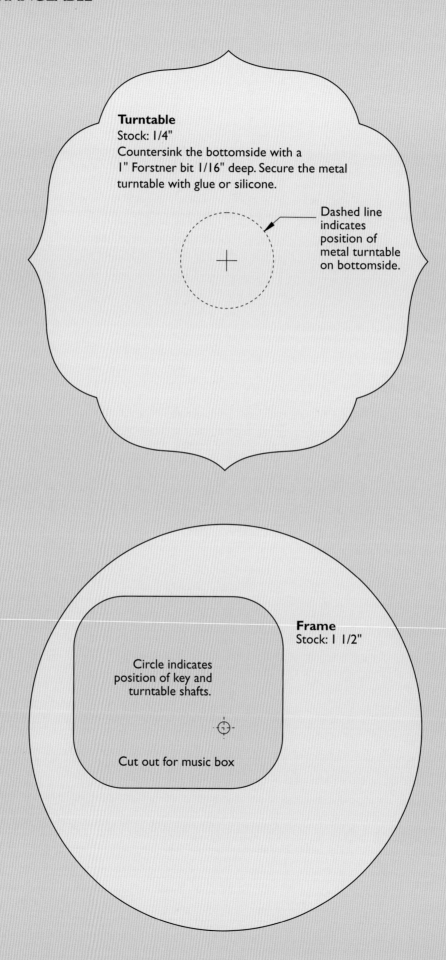

Turntable
Stock: 1/4"
Countersink the bottomside with a
1" Forstner bit 1/16" deep. Secure the metal
turntable with glue or silicone.

Dashed line
indicates
position of
metal turntable
on bottomside.

Frame
Stock: 1 1/2"

Circle indicates
position of key and
turntable shafts.

Cut out for music box

Design 2

Bird & Hearts
Stock: 3/8"

Cupid & Harp
Stock: 3/8"

Angel & Birds
Stock: 3/8"

Victorian Heart
Stock: 3/8"

Gal
Stock: 3/8"

Roses
Stock: 3/8"

Horse
Stock: 3/8"

Candles
Stock: 3/8"

Design 2

Angel
Stock: 3/8"

Singer
Stock: 3/8"

Flowers
Stock: 3/8"

Love Birds
Stock: 3/8"

Design 2

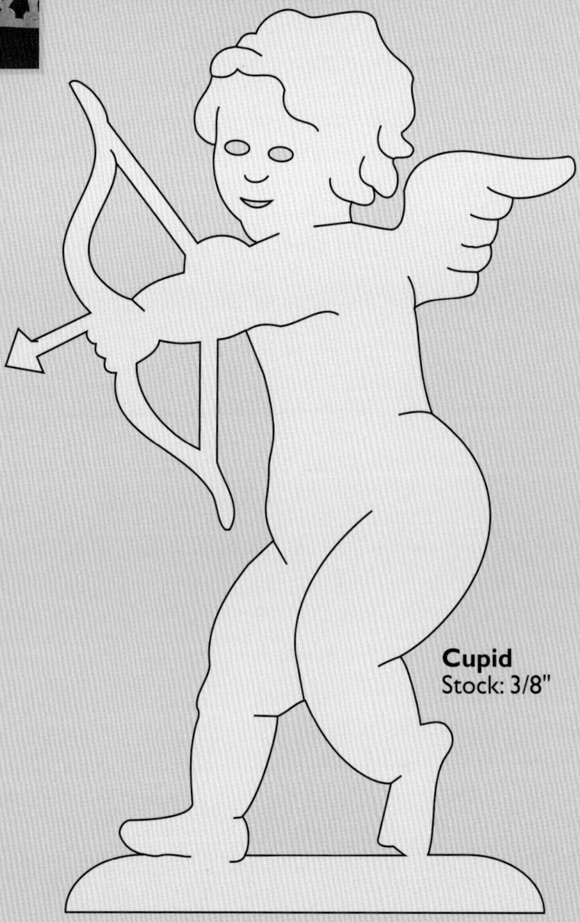

Cupid
Stock: 3/8"

Angel
Stock: 3/8"

Valentine
Stock: 3/8"

Messenger
Stock: 3/8"

Lady
Stock: 3/8"

Gentleman
Stock: 3/8"

Design 2

Flowery Heart
Stock: 3/8"

Sweet Couple
Stock: 3/8"

More Great Project Books from Fox Chapel Publishing

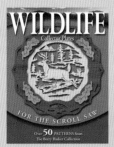

Wildlife Collector Plates for the Scroll Saw
Over 50 Patterns from The Berry Basket Collection
By Rick and Karen Longabaugh
$16.95
1-56523-300-X
128 pages

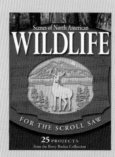

Scenes of North American Wildlife for the Scroll Saw
25 Projects from The Berry Basket Collection
By Rick and Karen Longabaugh
$16.95
1-56523-277-1
128 pages

Holiday Ornam⚫ for the Scroll Sa⚫
Over 300 Beautifu⚫ Patterns from The Berry Basket Collection
By Rick and Karen Longabaugh
$16.95
1-56523-276-3
120 pages

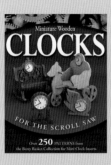

Miniature Wooden Clocks for the Scroll Saw
Over 250 Patterns from The Berry Basket Collection
By Rick and Karen Longabaugh
$16.95
1-56523-275-5
128 pages

Multi-Use Collapsible Basket Patterns
Over 100 Designs for the Scroll Saw
By Rick and Karen Longabaugh
$12.95
1-56523-088-4
128 pages

Custom Wooden Boxes for the S⚫ Saw
Innovative Techniq⚫ and Complete Plan⚫ 31 Projects
By Diana Thompson⚫
$17.95
1-56523-212-7
112 pages

LOOK FOR THESE BOOKS AT YOUR LOCAL BOOK STORE OR WOODWORKING RETAILER
Or call 800-457-9112 • Visit www.FoxChapelPublishing.com

Learn from the Experts

You already know that Fox Chapel Publishing is a leading source for woodworking books, videos, and DVDs, but did you know that we also publish *Scroll Saw Workshop*? Published quarterly, *Scroll Saw Workshop* is the magazine scroll saw enthusiasts turn to for the premium projects and expert information from today's leading wood crafters. Contact us today for your free trial issue!

Scroll Saw Work Shop

- Written by today's leading scroll saw artists
- Dozens of attractive, shop-tested patterns and project ideas for scrollers of all skill levels
- Great full-color photos of step-by-step projects and completed work-presented in a clear, easy-to-follow format
- Keep up with what's new in the scrolling community with tool reviews, artist profiles, and event coverage

Subscribe Today! 888-840-8590 • www.scrollsawer.com